Especially for

_____

From

_____

Date

_____

You Are
Blessed

with love Mike

You Are Blessed

Inspiration to Recharge Your Soul

Darlene Sala

BARBOUR
PUBLISHING

© 2008 by Darlene Sala

Readings originally published in the Philippines, under the title *Refreshing Words for Busy Women,* by OMF Literature, Inc.

Print ISBN 978-1-62416-132-2

eBook Editions:
Adobe Digital Edition (.epub) 978-1-62416-437-8
Kindle and MobiPocket Edition (.prc) 978-1-62416-436-1

Published by Barbour Publishing, Inc., P.O. Box 719, Uhrichsville, Ohio 44683, www.barbourbooks.com

Our mission is to publish and distribute inspirational products offering exceptional value and biblical encouragement to the masses.

Member of the
Evangelical Christian
Publishers Association

Printed in China.

*Dedicated to all busy women
who thirst for freshening,
invigorating, revitalizing,
restorative, health-giving
Living Water.*

Special thanks go to
Yna Reyes, Joanna Nicolas-Na,
Karen Huang, Marianne Ventura,
Lety Paler, Butch Pang,
my daughter Bonnie Craddick,
and my husband, Harold Sala.

BEFORE YOU BEGIN

E very woman I know is a busy woman—
that's the way life is in the twenty-first
century. All the more important, then, to
take daily breaks to "refresh your soul"
(Psalm 23:3). Not meant to be a substitute
for Bible study, these brief devotional selections are written to refresh and strengthen
you—and sometimes challenge you, as well.

Because the selections are all scripture-
based and encouraging, I hope they will be
for you like a drink of cool water when you
are thirsty and tired.

"I will refresh the weary
and satisfy the faint."
JEREMIAH 31:25

Commit to the LORD whatever you do,
and he will establish your plans.
PROVERBS 16:3

———————

A NEW PENCIL AND NOTEBOOK

When I was a kid, I always liked to get a brand-new pencil, sharpen it to a perfect point, and sit down with a fresh new notebook. Somehow that pristine pencil and paper presented so many possibilities. A New Year feels like this to me, too—a fresh beginning.

I remember sitting down at the start of one New Year and praying, "Lord, I want this whole year to make a difference for You." But the problem with that prayer is that I never experience the whole year in one instance. Every year comes in 365 days, each of which has 24 hours or 1,440 minutes. Unless I make those individual days and hours count for God, when December rolls around again, nothing will have changed.

Maybe one never gets to the place of total

24-hours-a-day commitment to God's will. My experience is that commitment only comes in moment-sized acts of obedience. I find no problem, personally, in committing the whole year to God—or my whole life, for that matter. It's the moments that give me trouble—the little decisions about the use of my time, money, and energy. The question is, what does God want me to do right now? Am I willing to do it?

Lord, beginning today, help me to look at each moment as important to You. Your Word says, "Commit to the LORD whatever you do" (Proverbs 16:3). Help me to care more about what You want than what I want. Thank You for the "new pencil and new notebook"—a fresh start.

Children, obey your parents in everything,
for this pleases the Lord.
COLOSSIANS 3:20

MY WILL—OR GOD'S?

One evening my daughter called my eldest grandson, who was just a toddler then, to come to the table for dinner. She was taken aback when he replied, "No, Mommy, I'm not going to come. I'm going to play now." As you can imagine, that day my grandson learned the meaning of the scripture verse that says, "Children, obey your parents in everything, for this pleases the Lord" (Colossians 3:20).

When my daughter told me about this, I felt a twinge of guilt. How many times have I said that to God when He spoke to my heart about something He wanted me to do? "No, Lord, I want to do something else right now." You see, there's another power in my life besides God—a strong one: it's my own will. While I hate to admit it, many times my will is against God's will. This battle for my own way is the essence of sin. Isaiah wrote, "We all, like sheep, have gone astray, each of us has turned to our own way" (Isaiah 53:6). My way as opposed to God's way. I have been given the ability to make the choice.

Every day I need to come to the Lord and ask, "What do You want me to do today?" Romans 12 tells us to present our bodies as a living sacrifice to the Lord. But as someone pointed out, the problem with living sacrifices is that they keep crawling off the altar. That's why I find I need to present myself to the Lord every day.

Which will it be today—God's will or yours?

3

Peter got down out of the boat, walked on the water and came toward Jesus. But when he saw the wind, he was afraid and, beginning to sink, cried out, "Lord, save me!"

MATTHEW 14:29–30
(THE WHOLE STORY: MATTHEW 14:22–33)

WHAT ARE YOU LOOKING AT?

I'm so glad Jesus chose Peter to be one of His disciples, because he's like most of us—curious, impetuous, and sometimes weak.

Matthew 14 tells us the story of one of the best-known events in Peter's life. The disciples were in a boat, and Jesus came to them walking on the water. They thought he was a ghost, but Jesus immediately said, "Take courage! It is I. Don't be afraid" (verse 27).

"Lord, if it's you," Peter replied, "tell me to come to you on the water." Jesus said, "Come," so Peter audaciously got out of the boat and walked on the water toward Jesus. When he saw the storm, however, he began to sink.

Immediately Jesus reached out and caught him. As long as Peter's eyes were on Jesus, he walked on water. But when he looked at the circumstances around him, he began to sink.

When you focus your attention on how many bills you have to pay or the doctor's diagnosis of leukemia, like Peter, you'll begin to sink. Where you focus your attention makes all the difference. If you look in your own heart, you'll become depressed. If you look back to your past, you'll feel defeated by the memory of failures. If you look to others, you may be disappointed. But if you look to Christ, you will never be depressed or defeated or disappointed.

"Fixing our eyes on Jesus, the pioneer and perfecter of faith," says Hebrews 12:2. When you're overwhelmed by the storm, look to Jesus. He is there. Reach for His hand.

4

Your hands made me and formed me.
PSALM 119:73

THE SHAPE I'M IN

Most of us are not happy with our bodies. We'd like to shed a few pounds—without effort, of course. We wish we had firmer muscles or shapelier curves. But what we have is what we've got, right?

Now, the Bible says in the beginning God formed Adam "from the dust of the ground" (Genesis 2:7). But He formed you, too. The psalmist echoed, "Your hands made me and formed me" (Psalm 119:73).

So if God formed you, what does that tell you about your body? Clearly, that your body is exactly what God intended for you, to accomplish His unique purpose. We can't blame God when we don't take care of ourselves. Because our bodies are tools God has given us to serve Him, we should take care of them for His purposes.

What if you are disabled? Does God still have a purpose for you? Absolutely. When she was a teen, poet Annie Johnson Flint developed crippling arthritis that worsened until her later years; a pencil had to be wedged between her fingers for her to write. Yet she authored more than seven volumes of poetry that have no trace of self-pity or railing against God's will. She wrote,

God hath not promised skies always blue,
Flower strewn pathways all our lives through;
But God hath promised strength for the day,
Rest for the labor, light for the way.[1]

Offer your body to the Lord today as a gift, "holy and pleasing to God" (Romans 12:1). You'll be amazed with what He does with it.

[1]http://www.hymnal.net/hymn.php?t=nt&n=720 accessed September 10, 2008.

Brethren, I count not myself to have apprehended: but this one thing I do....
PHILIPPIANS 3:13 KJV

THIS ONE THING I DO

My friend Georgalyn has always been an extremely busy lady. When her husband died at a young age, she raised their two young daughters alone. Through those years and until now, she has also headed one Christian organization or another. At one time it was missionary radio, and now it is missionary printing. With her compassion for needy people, she makes a difference with her life.

While I've always admired her spunk and dedication, I observed something else in Georgalyn that spoke to my heart in a special way. Busy as she was, she made a decision to always give herself totally to her present task. For instance, whenever someone stopped her to talk, she would really listen. No matter how busy she was or how many things she had on her mind, she would give her undivided attention to that person.

The apostle Paul said, "This one thing I do" (Philippians 3:13 KJV). When you get right down to it, that's about all most of us can handle well at any one time anyway, isn't it? One thing at a time.

Jesus was the master of this. I'm sure that no matter whom He talked to, that person knew he had Jesus' undivided attention. He took time to meet each need before He went on to the next. And no one else had more people demanding His attention than Jesus did!

"This one thing I do"—may God help us to remember this thought today and put it into practice. Just maybe it will become a habit.

6

"I will surely bless you and make your descendants as numerous as the stars in the sky."
GENESIS 22:17

HOW MANY STARS?

In the year 125 BC, Hipparchus counted the number of stars in the heavens. He concluded that there were 1,022. Seventy-five years later, however, the astronomer Ptolemy found four more and declared that there were 1,026.

Interestingly enough, the Bible, written 2,700 years *before* Ptolemy, said that the stars were innumerable. God promised Abraham that his descendants would be "as numerous as the stars in the sky and as the sand on the seashore" (Genesis 22:17). Skeptics scoffed at such a comparison. To compare the number of stars to grains of sand on the seashore was laughable. After all, there are more grains in a handful of sand than the 1,026 stars Ptolemy claimed existed.

But only a few years ago on a highly acclaimed television program the noted evolutionary scientist Carl Sagan said there are probably about as many stars in the sky as there are grains of sand on the seashores of the world. The Bible, written centuries ago, has been correct all along.

Psalm 147:4 tells us, "He [God] determines the number of the stars and calls them each by name." We humans haven't yet counted them all, let alone named each star. But God has already counted and named each of them.

It's no wonder the psalmist wrote, "When I consider. . .the stars, which you have set in place, what is mankind that you are mindful of them, human beings that you care for them?" (Psalm 8:3–4).

7

Jesus answered, "It is written: 'Man shall not live on bread alone, but on every word that comes from the mouth of God.'"

MATTHEW 4:4

THE INSTRUCTION BOOK

When you buy a machine—whether it's a computer, a car, or a sewing machine—you receive a book of instructions. Most of us set this book aside, doubting we'll ever use it. But one day when something goes wrong with your equipment, you may wonder, *Where is that instruction book that came with this?*

You know that old saying, "If all else fails, read the instructions"? Well, we'd say a person is not very wise if he knows nothing about a piece of equipment and yet refuses to refer to the directions on how to use it. Yet many people never open the instruction book that tells how to fix a human being—the Bible. It's the book that tells where we came from, what we were made for, how we can be kept in working order—in fact, exactly what will make us most useful and effective. The great tragedy is that so many people try to live their lives without *the* instruction book.

Jesus said, "Man shall not live on bread alone, but on every word that comes from the mouth of God" (Matthew 4:4). If you've never opened a Bible, I'd suggest beginning with the book of Mark in the New Testament. For one thing, it's short and to the point. You'll get an overview of who Jesus is and why He came to earth. Mark those verses that speak to your heart.

You will be surprised how practical God's instruction book is. Not only will you find directions on how to live, you'll meet the One who designed you—and He can fix anything.

But Moses said to God, "Who am I that I should go to Pharaoh and bring the Israelites out of Egypt?"

EXODUS 3:11

(THE WHOLE STORY: EXODUS 3:1–22)

WHO AM I?

The bush was on fire but it wasn't being burned up. Curious, Moses stopped to investigate. Never in a thousand years did he expect to hear what he heard—God's voice speaking aloud to him, telling him that he had been commissioned to lead the Israelites out of slavery in Egypt to the place God had promised would be their homeland.

Moses' immediate response was one of utter shock! "Who am I to do a job like that?" he asked. "Don't You remember I had to make a fast getaway out of Egypt because they wanted to kill me there? Now You want me to go back and talk Pharaoh into letting his labor force quit?"

Maybe God is speaking to your heart about something He wants you to do—something you feel is totally beyond your ability. Like Moses, you are saying, "Who am I to take on a job like that?" God reminded Moses that His name is "I AM"—that He is the God of the past, present, and future. He is the God of *your* past, *your* present, and *your* future.

When God gives you a job to do, what matters most is not who you are, but who God is. He will stand behind you with the resources you need to carry out the task He gives you— whether it's a new job, a special call to ministry, or sharing the Gospel with your coworker in the office. Don't worry about who you are; remember who God is—the great ever-present One, who will go with you as you do what He has called you to do.

*When I said, My foot slippeth; thy mercy,
O LORD, held me up. In the multitude of my
thoughts within me thy comforts delight my soul.*
PSALM 94:18–19 KJV

THE GOD OF ALL COMFORT

*C*omfort. It's a word I like to hear. It has such
a—well, reassuring sound to it. It's also a
Bible word. In just five verses of one chapter,
2 Corinthians 1, the word *comfort* occurs in
some form seven times.

Let me give you a sample from 2 Corinthians
1:3–4: "Praise be to the God and Father of our
Lord Jesus Christ, the Father of compassion and
the God of all comfort, who comforts us in all our
troubles." That's beautiful, isn't it?

The idea is more than just that He
consoles us when we're sad or upset. Bible
teacher G. Campbell Morgan writes,

*It is the great thought of underpinned,
strengthened comradeship, being by the side*

of, upholding. That is the great word, the upholding power that comes from God.[1]

It's not a sign of weakness to admit you need God's help. In fact, it would be foolish to try to get through life without Him. When life piles up on us, when we face grief and difficulty, we need to turn to our Comforter. The psalmist wrote, "When I said, 'My foot is slipping,' your unfailing love, LORD, supported me. When anxiety was great within me, your consolation brought me joy" (Psalm 94:18–19).

Many years before Christ was born, the prophet Isaiah said that God would be sending Christ to earth "to bind up the brokenhearted" (Isaiah 61:1). Do you need Him to bind up your broken heart today? He is the great Comforter who will come to your side and walk with you through difficult days.

[1]G. Campbell Morgan, *The Corinthian Letters of Paul* (Grand Rapids, MI: Fleming H. Revell Company, 1946), 227.

*I will instruct you and teach you in
the way you should go; I will counsel
you with my loving eye on you.*
PSALM 32:8

GOD'S GENTLE PUSHES

My dad used to tell people of an incident that happened when our family was traveling some distance by car. It was long before the days of seat belts, and I was standing in the front seat between them. I was about four years old, and I was whistling. My mom had had ear trouble as a child, and just a sharp whistle would cause pain in her ears, so she gave me a little poke in the side with her elbow.

My dad says I immediately looked at him and with a grin said, "Daddy, I can read Mama's pushes. That one meant stop whistling." He said they laughed about it, but as he drove, he thought, *Dear Lord, I wish I were as sensitive to Your gentle pushes, so that You would not have to deal with me harshly in order for me to know what You want me to do.*

God says in Psalm 32:8, "I will instruct you and teach you in the way you should go." It is possible to have such a sensitive heart that God can communicate His will to us without having to put a major roadblock in our path to get our attention. Isaiah says, "Whether you turn to the right or to the left, your ears will hear a voice behind you, saying, 'This is the way; walk in it'" (Isaiah 30:21).

Has God been giving you one of His gentle pushes? If so, you know what He wants you to do. So why don't you act on it today?

11

*This poor man called, and the L*ORD *heard him;*
he saved him out of all his troubles.

PSALM 34:6

R. A. TORREY'S CONVERSION

When R. A. Torrey was a young man, he had no faith in God or the Bible. His mother, an earnest Christian, pleaded with him to turn to God.

One day he said to her, "I don't want to hear any more about my sins and your prayers. I'm leaving." His weeping mother responded, "Son, you are going the wrong way. But when you come to your darkest hour, if you earnestly call on your mother's God and seek Him with all your heart, you will get the help you need."

Torrey went deeper and deeper into sin. At last one night, weary of life, with problems pressing down on him, he decided, *I'll take that gun I have in the drawer, and end my life.*

But his mother's words came rushing back to him. Convicted, he desperately cried out,

"O God of my mother, if there be such a Being, I need help. I need light. If You will give it to me, I will follow You."

With tears running down his face, he put his trust in Christ as his Savior. Torrey's dark heart was filled with the light of God's love. He then hurried home to tell his mother that her prayers had been answered. Reuben A. Torrey became an outstanding evangelist and helped win thousands to Christ. He founded the Bible Institute of Los Angeles—now known as Biola University, one of the leading Christian universities in the United States.

Torrey learned the reality of the scripture that says, "This poor man called, and the Lord heard him; he saved him out of all his troubles" (Psalm 34:6). The God who saved Torrey will save you as well!

12

Where can I go from your Spirit?
Where can I flee from your presence?
PSALM 139:7
(THE WHOLE STORY: PSALM 139:7–12)

WHEREVER YOU GO, THERE YOU ARE

Wherever you go, there you are."
What a silly saying, I thought. Of course wherever you go, there you are. Where else would you be?

But then I thought of how people try to escape from themselves and their troubles. They move to another place, thinking everything will be different there. Before long, they find the same old problems—alcohol addiction, marital troubles, busyness. That's because when they moved, they brought themselves with them. It's true—wherever you go, there you are.

There's the ultimate attempt to escape—suicide, but that only brings you face-to-face with the other Person you cannot escape from—God. David said,

Where can I go from your Spirit?
Where can I flee from your presence?
If I go up to the heavens, you are there;
   if I make my bed in the depths,
   you are there.
If I rise on the wings of the dawn,
   if I settle on the far side of the sea,
   even there your hand will guide me,
   your right hand will hold me fast.
If I say, "Surely the darkness will hide me
   and the light become night around me,"
   even the darkness will not be dark to you;
   the night will shine like the day,
For darkness is as light to you.
PSALM 139:7–12

There's only one way out of this dilemma:
Come to God just as you are. Confess your
shortcomings and failures; for He paid for your
sins on the cross, and He offers forgiveness.
"Therefore, since we have been justified
through faith, we have peace with God through
our Lord Jesus Christ" (Romans 5:1). Peace
with God brings peace with yourself, too. You
can stop running away.

13

*"So don't be afraid; you are
worth more than many sparrows."*
MATTHEW 10:31
(THE WHOLE STORY: MATTHEW 10:26–33)

LESSONS FROM SPARROWS

When Jesus talked about God's care for the birds, He chose the humble sparrow as His illustration. That's an interesting choice, for sparrows are one of the most common birds on earth. Some people even consider them pests.

Sparrows live almost exclusively among people. According to one study, wherever the number of households increases, the sparrow population increases proportionately. Sparrows build their nests under the eaves of houses; inside shutter boxes; in holes in a wall; or in places such as parks, close to where people live.

From ancient times, sparrows have appeared in folklore, fairy tales, and proverbs. Because sparrows are so common, Jesus knew that through the centuries people would read His words and relate.

Jesus said, "Are not two sparrows sold for a penny? Yet not one of them will fall to the ground outside your Father's care. . . . So don't be afraid; you are worth more than many sparrows" (Matthew 10:29, 31). It's significant that Jesus would take note of their death since the sparrow lives only a few years.

Jesus added, "Look at the birds of the air; they do not sow or reap or store away in barns, and yet your heavenly Father feeds them. Are you not much more valuable than they? . . . So do not worry. . . . But seek first his kingdom and his righteousness, and all these things will be given to you as well" (Matthew 6:26, 31, 33). He cares for the little sparrow; imagine how much more He cares for you.

14

Submit yourselves, then, to God.
Resist the devil, and he will flee from you.
JAMES 4:7

WHEN YOU DON'T WANT
TO DO SOMETHING

What happens when you know God wants you to do something but you don't want to do it?

Let's say that you have a friend who is sick. She *really* is your good friend, but every time you call her, she talks and talks and talks. You know God wants you to call her, but if you do, you'll be on the phone for hours. Do you:

1. Make excuses? "I can't call her today. If I do, I won't have enough time to read my Bible."
2. Rationalize? "She's probably so sick she doesn't feel like talking to me anyway."

3. Procrastinate? "I'm just too tired. I'll call her first thing tomorrow morning. I really will."

Think about an area in your life where you don't want to obey God. You know what? The devil doesn't want you to obey God either.

If you are having a hard time obeying God, James has the answer. He says, "Submit yourselves, then, to God. Resist the devil, and he will flee from you" (James 4:7). We have the mistaken idea that God and the devil are equal powers. Not so. Remember, Christ has already defeated the devil. He's sentenced and just waiting for execution. If you are a believer in Jesus Christ, God lives in you. You have the power to resist Satan, and God's promise is that Satan will flee.

When you don't want to do something you know you should do, stand firm against the devil and then submit to God. When you do, you will find the power to do that difficult thing He is asking you.

15

*"Return home and tell how
much God has done for you."*
LUKE 8:39
(THE WHOLE STORY: LUKE 8:26–39)

TELL HOW MUCH GOD
HAS DONE FOR YOU

After crossing the Sea of Galilee Jesus
stepped onshore and was immediately
confronted by a man possessed by demons. The
Bible tells us: "For a long time this man had not
worn clothes or lived in a house, but had lived in
the tombs" (Luke 8:27). The local people had
tried to chain him and keep him under guard,
but he always broke the chains and escaped.

To make a long story short, Jesus cast the
demons out of the man. The townspeople
found him later, dressed and calmly sitting at
Jesus' feet, in his right mind and begging to go
with Jesus. "No," Jesus said. "Return home
and tell how much God has done for you"
(Luke 8:39).

I, for one, would like to have sat at his dinner table that night and listened to him tell all the details of the story.

Think of how much God has done for you. Have you shared the details with your family recently? Tell them how God protected you when you had that close call in heavy traffic. Or perhaps how He met the urgent financial need that had been worrying you or answered a request you'd been praying about for weeks. Or how at last, you had a chance to share Christ with your boss at work.

Tonight, why don't *you* "return home and tell how much God has done for you"? Don't keep good news to yourself. Share it with your family. You will bless them and bring praise to God for His mighty power.

*Then you will call, and the LORD will answer;
you will cry for help, and he will say: Here am I.*
ISAIAH 58:9

(THE WHOLE STORY: ISAIAH 58:6–11)

PERSPECTIVE

For a moment, pretend that you are God and you're listening to these prayers:

"O Lord, help Danny to be the high-scorer at the basketball game tonight so he can get the MVP trophy!"

What a contrast to this one: "O Lord, send us money so Danny can go to school!"

Or one family prays, "Please, God, give us sunny weather for our cruise!" while another prays, "Please, God, send rain to save our crops!"

"God, please help me lose weight so I can wear that beautiful dress to the party," a young mom prays, while another pleads, "Please, God, send us food so I can feed my family."

If you were God, it's not hard to figure out

which prayers you would want to answer first, is it? Now, is it wrong to pray for good weather for your vacation or for a successful career? No, of course not. But when we get a bit demanding with God and disappointed when He doesn't give us every luxury we want, it's time to get life back in perspective.

In the Bible we're told to pray about everything, and I believe that means exactly what it says—*everything*. But don't confuse that with thinking that we *need* everything. I think God must sometimes shake His head and smile when He hears what we who have so much think our needs are.

So go ahead and pray about everything—absolutely everything. But remember that it's our needs that God has promised to supply when we are obedient to Him. The Bible says, "The LORD will guide you always; he will satisfy your needs" (Isaiah 58:11).

By faith the prostitute Rahab,
because she welcomed the spies, was not
killed with those who were disobedient.

Hebrews 11:31

(the whole story: Hebrews 11:1–40)

Woman of Faith

The Bible has its own "Hall of Fame": Hebrews 11. It's a list of people famous for believing and trusting God. You'd expect to find Abraham and Moses there, but you may be surprised to see a woman listed who was not exactly chairman of the Spiritual Life Committee of her church. In fact, she was a prostitute. Her name was Rahab.

Obviously Rahab didn't get there on the basis of purity—but then, which of us could? Here's the story: Joshua sent two spies to Jericho to assess the city before attacking. Probably in order not to arouse suspicion, the men went to Rahab's house. But word leaked out to the king, who demanded that Rahab hand over the spies. She admitted they had been there but said they already fled. Actually, she had hidden them under stalks of flax on her rooftop.

That evening Rahab told Joshua's men, "I know that the LORD has given you this land ....for the LORD your God is God in heaven above and on the earth below" (Joshua 2:9, 11). Then she boldly asked that she and her family be spared when the Israelites attacked. And indeed, "By faith the prostitute Rahab, because she welcomed the spies, was not killed with those who were disobedient" (Hebrews 11:31). Rahab had a faith that gave her daring courage and earned her a place among the famous who believed God.

Rahab's fame doesn't end there. Her great-great grandson was King David, placing her in the lineage of Jesus Himself (Matthew 1:5–6). Now that's an honor!

No, you don't have to be "perfect" to be used by God—just willing and available.

*That is, that you and I may be mutually
encouraged by each other's faith.*

ROMANS 1:12

ENCOURAGING ONE ANOTHER

Sometimes I don't think we fully realize how much we encourage one another when we share about the good things God has done in our lives. I, for one, love to get a phone call or an e-mail telling me how God has met a need in a friend's life or answered a prayer. That encourages me to keep on praying until He does the same in my life. To the Christians in Rome Paul talked about being "mutually encouraged by each other's faith" (Romans 1:12).

It's especially good to talk to our families about what the Lord has done. Moses told the people, "Be careful, and watch yourselves closely so that you do not forget the things your eyes have seen or let them fade from your heart as long as you live. Teach them to your children and to their children after them" (Deuteronomy 4:9).

I guess sometimes we're hesitant to talk about what God has done in our lives because we're afraid people will think we're trying to impress them with how spiritual we are. Don't let those fears stop you. You know that it's a great encouragement in your walk with God when someone shares with you, so don't hesitate to return the favor.

Psalm 126:3 says, "The LORD has done great things for us, and we are filled with joy." Find someone today who needs to be encouraged. Talk about the great goodness of the Lord. I think you will find, as Romans 1:12 says, that you are "mutually encouraged by each other's faith."

Taste and see that the LORD is good;
blessed is the one who takes refuge in him.
PSALM 34:8

THE CHALLENGE OF ILLNESS

A plaque hanging on a hospital wall puts it well:

Cancer is so limited. . . .
It cannot cripple love.
It cannot shatter hope.
It cannot corrode faith. . .destroy peace . . .
   [or] kill friendships.
It cannot suppress memories. . .
   silence courage. . .[or] invade the soul.
It cannot steal eternal life.
It cannot conquer the spirit.

My friend Louise is fighting cancer. Every three weeks she has chemotherapy that lasts the entire day and leaves her debilitated.

Yes, she gets discouraged. Numbness

in her fingers and toes and the pains that accompany this treatment are certainly draining. Not one to let grass grow under her feet, she finds it hard when she doesn't have the energy to do all the things she wants to do.

But Louise is a believer in Jesus. God's Spirit in her life is evidenced by love, faith, hope, peace, friendship, courage, and a conquering spirit. She wastes little time on questions like, "Why is this happening to me?" Instead, she says,

> *I know who holds my tomorrows, and I know who holds my hand today! I praise God for the wonderful peace He gives me deep inside and for His wonderful people who walk alongside and encourage me when my body grows tired! While I am walking through the valley of the shadow of death, I know it is just a shadow, because the reality of the living Christ is with me, and His joy is my strength.*

And then she adds, "I suggest you taste and see how good the Lord really is," echoing Psalm 34:8. Meaningful advice from someone who speaks from experience.

He is our God and we are the people of his pasture, the flock under his care.
PSALM 95:7

DON'T YOU CARE?

The sky above the Sea of Galilee was already dark when a squall came up. Waves began to break over the boat so that it was nearly swamped. During all this Jesus was asleep on a cushion at the back of the boat. The disciples woke Him, shouting over the howling winds, "Teacher, don't you care if we drown?" Jesus "got up. . .and said to the waves, 'Quiet! Be still!'. . .and it was completely calm" (Mark 4:38–39).

Did Jesus not care about the disciples when the storm was raging? Of course He did. It's just that He knew all along that they would safely reach the other side. But only when the disciples could see the evidence did they have peace that everything was going to be all right.

Like the disciples, we ask, "Lord, don't You

care?" In other words, "Aren't You going to do something about my predicament?" We ask those words when we're in a situation where we can see no logical explanation. And the answer? Yes, God does care. Psalm 95 says, "For he is our God and we are the people of his pasture, the flock under his care" (Psalm 95:7).

Whether you're in a storm that seems like it's going to overwhelm you, or you're frustrated because you're working hard and no one cares, or the rent is due and there's no way to pay it, realize God sees and cares. Jesus speaks to you those words, "Quiet! Be still!"

"Cast all your anxiety on him because he cares for you" (1 Peter 5:7). Hold on for just a little longer. Later you'll understand how great is His care for you.

*"Anyone who chooses to do the will of God
will find out whether my teaching comes
from God or whether I speak on my own."*
JOHN 7:17

HOW TO KNOW

The first four books of the New Testament
contain pages and pages of the teachings
of Jesus. Do you want to know if all that Jesus
said is true? Jesus Himself told us how to find
out. He said in John, the fourth book of the
New Testament, "Anyone who chooses to
do the will of God will find out whether my
teaching comes from God or whether I speak
on my own" (John 7:17).

Sounds pretty simple, doesn't it? If you
choose to do God's will, you'll know if what
Jesus says is really from God. You may have
heard that the Bible is a good book. You may
even have read some of it. But you may wonder
if what it says is true. Then ask yourself this
question: "Do I really want to do God's will?"

If that is your attitude, then sit down with a Bible, open it to the beginning of John, and start reading. While you are reading, keep in mind that you're looking for truth, and Jesus will reveal Himself through His Word. He said that when you choose to do His will, you will know if what He said is true or not.

Brother Yun, a famous Chinese pastor often called "The Heavenly Man," said: "You can never really know the scriptures until you are willing to be changed by them." With this in mind, ask yourself, "Am I willing?" If so, you are about to embark on the greatest adventure of your life.

22

A great and powerful wind tore the mountains apart and shattered the rocks before the LORD, but the LORD was not in the wind. After the wind there was an earthquake, but the LORD was not in the earthquake. After the earthquake came a fire, but the LORD was not in the fire. And after the fire came a gentle whisper.

1 KINGS 19:11–12

(THE WHOLE STORY: 1 KINGS 19:1–18)

A FAST FROM NOISE

Although not commanded directly in the Bible, you find many mentions of fasting, including Jesus' instruction about not doing it in a way that would attract people's attention.

But author Dr. Terry Teykl recommends a fast that would do many of us a lot of good. It's a fast not from food, but from noise. Isn't that an interesting thought? He writes,

> *Decide to embark on a special kind of fast— giving up unnecessary noise and activity. Say to yourself, "I will embrace solitude."[1]*

Sometime today stop long enough to really listen to what is going on around you. You may hear voices, traffic, a radio or TV, possibly the sounds of machinery running. Every day we're surrounded with unending noise.

If you set aside some time for solitude and quiet, however, you will find a fresh awareness of the presence of God. You will also find new strength, for Isaiah 30:15 says, "In quietness and trust is your strength."

There is, however, a sure way to promote God's absence, writes C. S. Lewis: "Avoid silence. . . . Concentrate on money, sex, status, health, and (above all) on your grievances. Keep the radio on. Live in a crowd."[2]

There is a lot in this life that would drown out God's voice. If you're experiencing that problem, consider a fast from noise for even thirty minutes. Use earplugs if you need to. Then listen for the still, small voice of God. First Kings 19 says He sometimes speaks to us in a gentle whisper.

[1]Dr. Terry Teykl, *The Lighthouse Devotional* (Sisters, OR: Multnomah Publishers, 2000), 220.

[2]C. S. Lewis, "The Seeing Eye," in *Lewis: Christian Reflections,* ed. Walter Hooper (Grand Rapids, MI: Eerdmans, 1975), 168–169.

23

Let us continually offer to
God a sacrifice of praise.
HEBREWS 13:15

WHEN CLOUDS OF DEPRESSION COME

Some parts of the Bible are easy to read but hard to put into practice. Take Hebrews 13:15–16, for instance: "Let us continually offer to God a sacrifice of praise—the fruit of lips that openly profess his name. And do not forget to do good and to share with others, for with such sacrifices God is pleased."

Obeying those instructions is easy when I'm in a good mood and everything is going smoothly. Yes, praising God and doing good to others is a joy when the sun is shining. But when I'm depressed, I forget to praise the Lord, I'm not apt to think about the needs of others, and I don't really want to share.

What would happen if a depressed person actually followed those three Bible instructions?

1. Continually offer praise to the Lord.
2. Do good deeds.
3. Share with others.

You may be thinking, *It's not possible for a clinically depressed person to do these things,* and maybe you're right. But when most of us get depressed, we *could* do something about it if we wanted to. We're depressed and don't praise God because we don't like our circumstances; we're too focused on what's happening to us.

Yet when I praise the Lord, my mood becomes lighter. When I do something kind, I'm blessed myself. Sharing gets me out of my self-centeredness.

Start with offering a sacrifice of praise to the Lord right now—whether you feel like it or not. Steps 2 and 3—good deeds and sharing— will then be a lot easier.

24

"Will not God bring about justice for his chosen ones, who cry out to him day and night? Will he keep putting them off?"

LUKE 18:7

(THE WHOLE STORY: LUKE 18:1–8)

POSSIBLE OR IMPOSSIBLE?

Those difficult circumstances you're dealing with right now—how do you see them? As insurmountable? Or as an opportunity for God to do the impossible?

It's amazing what a difference attitude makes. For years my husband has had a sign in his office that says, "Don't tell me that it can't be done. Tell me how we'll do it." Sometimes what we need to do is simply get our eyes off the difficulties and focus instead on what we can do to improve a situation.

But most times we need something more.

William Carey knew he needed something more. Throughout his forty-one years of missionary work in India, he faced many insurmountable obstacles. But he continued to press on. He said, "You have not tested the resources of God until you attempt the impossible." I like that, because it challenges my faith. If you want to bolster your own faith, read his biography and you'll find that he proved by his life that God can do the impossible. Today, Carey is known as the "Father of Modern Missions."

Right now when you pray about that overwhelming situation you're facing, don't worry that you're asking for too much. Pray big prayers because we have a big God—one who truly does the impossible.

25

*You are judging by appearances. If anyone
is confident that they belong to Christ,
they should consider again that we belong
to Christ just as much as they do.*

2 CORINTHIANS 10:7

_____

DEFEATING DISCOURAGEMENT

Does this scenario fit you? Everything
seems to have gone wrong lately. Your job
is shaky, your health isn't great, your family has
problems, and your finances—well, let's just
say your bank account has acute anemia. You
can relate to the person who prayed, "Lord, if
there's any more trouble coming, send it now
while I'm used to it!"[1]

What do your circumstances tell you?
That there's no hope, right? But the apostle
Paul said, "You are judging by appearances"
(2 Corinthians 10:7).

"What do you mean, Paul? The facts are
pretty plain—I'm in deep trouble!"

Yes, you are, and you're discouraged. But

you may be overlooking the weapon God has given you to fight discouragement. It's the sword of the Spirit, which is the Word of God (Ephesians 6:17).

Sometimes we get so discouraged that we don't take hold of God's promises. When Moses told the Israelites that God was going to deliver them from Egyptian slavery, "they did not listen to him because of their discouragement" (Exodus 6:9). When depressed, we don't hear God's whispered promises of help.

But God's promises are true no matter how we feel. "The LORD himself goes before you and will be with you; he will never leave you nor forsake you. Do not be afraid; do not be discouraged" (Deuteronomy 31:8).

God's promises are the weapons He has given us to fight discouragement and renew hope. Search them out in scripture. In faith, set your mind on His promises today. God will meet you.

[1]Ray Pritchard, *The Healing Power of Forgiveness* (Eugene, OR: Harvest House Publishers, 2005), 131.

26

*For this is what the high and exalted
One says—he who lives forever, whose name
is holy: "I live in a high and holy place,
but also with the one who is contrite and lowly
in spirit, to revive the spirit of the lowly
and to revive the heart of the contrite."*
ISAIAH 57:15

DOES GOD FEEL AT HOME
IN YOUR THOUGHTS?

A. W. Tozer was a Bible teacher of the
last century. A deep thinker whose
books challenge the most experienced Bible
expositors, Tozer yet expressed his thoughts in
practical ways.

He was always keenly aware of the holiness
of God. Isaiah 57:15 made such an impact on
him: "For this is what the high and exalted One
says—he who lives forever, whose name is holy:
'I live in a high and holy place, but also with the
one who is contrite and lowly in spirit.' "

Tozer wrote,

God has been saying to me, "I dwell in your thoughts. Make your thoughts a sanctuary in which I can dwell."[1]

If you compare your life to a cathedral, your theology is the foundation, says Tozer, but your thoughts are the high bell tower. Make sure they are a place where God can feel at home.

Having thoughts that make God feel at home is a significant concept—and a practical one. We are what we think. If our thoughts are pleasing to the Lord, so will our lives be.

So, does that mean you should *always* be thinking lofty thoughts about God? The answer is clearly no. Isaiah tells us God lives in a high and holy place, the high bell tower, so to speak, "but also with the one who is contrite and lowly in spirit." A humble attitude of simple dependence on our holy God keeps us in fellowship with Him through the ordinary hours of our day.

Welcome God to the bell tower of your life.

[1] A. W. Tozer, *Tozer on Worship and Entertainment,* compiled by James L. Snyder (Camp Hill, PA: Christian Publications, 1998), 10–11.

27

*"Indeed, the very hairs of your head
are all numbered. Don't be afraid;
you are worth more than many sparrows."*
LUKE 12:7

THE BEANS IN OUR BIN

I'm always amazed when I remember that Jesus said, "Indeed, the very hairs of your head are all numbered" (Luke 12:7). My friend LuAnne learned that hairs aren't the only thing God keeps track of. Recently I received from her this urgent prayer request:

> *My husband, Bill, just came in and was very distraught. We have a grain bin that has $60,000 worth of soy beans in it. He just discovered that it has sprung a leak, and the top layer is rotten. He doesn't know how deep it has gone, but it is bad. The profit from those beans is what we will use to plant our crops next year. If we lose them, we will have to stop farming. Tomorrow he*

will get two men to go into the bin and scoop out the rotten beans.

The next day I received a second e-mail from her:

Thanks so much for lifting our needs to the Lord. As to the loss, it is several hundred bushels, and when we sell the rest, they will be discounted. Now we wait to see what the buyer says.

Within three days I heard from LuAnne again:

Today we took the first load of beans to the market. They took them at full price. We expected them to have a little mold on them, but they didn't. That was a miracle only the Lord could have done. He not only knows the hairs on our heads, but the beans in our bin.

Yes, God keeps track of hairs and beans and bank accounts, too. You can trust Him to keep track of all that matters to you!

28

*So we rebuilt the wall till all of
it reached half its height, for the
people worked with all their heart.*

NEHEMIAH 4:6

(THE WHOLE STORY: NEHEMIAH 2–3)

GETTING THE JOB DONE

In the fifth century BC, the walls of Jerusalem
lay in disrepair. So broken down were they
that the city had no protection. But under
Nehemiah, the people were challenged to do
something about the problem.

If the project were carried out today,
a contractor and professional stone layers
would be hired. But that wasn't an option in
Nehemiah's day. The only way the wall was
going to be rebuilt was for a large number
of able-bodied people to pitch in. The work
required people from nearby areas, too—not
just the residents of Jerusalem but citizens
from surrounding cities such as Jericho, Tekoa,
Gibeon, and Mizpah.

What an interesting group of workers from all walks of life! Some were merchants, some rulers, and others were priests who ordinarily did work in the temple. Two of the most unlikely laborers were Uzziel, a goldsmith, and Hananiah, a perfume maker. And men were not the only workers. Shallum repaired a section with the help of his daughters.

In just fifty-two days, the work was completed—in spite of criticism, ridicule, interference, and even a death threat on Nehemiah. Nehemiah gave credit to God for His help and to those who participated, for as Nehemiah put it, "the people had a mind to work" (Nehemiah 4:6 NASB).

I don't know what job needs to be done where you live, but for a training manual on how to do it, read the book of Nehemiah.

29

*Do everything without
grumbling or arguing.*
PHILIPPIANS 2:14

TRY THIS FOR ONE WEEK

Just six little words, that's all—but they're
powerful!

Here they are: "Do everything without
grumbling or arguing" (Philippians 2:14).

Six words simple to understand, but oh so
hard to do! If you don't think so, I challenge
you to put them into practice just for today:

1. Don't complain about anything.
2. Don't argue about anything.

How far do you think you'll get into your
day before you flunk the challenge? Can you
finish breakfast without complaining or arguing?
For some of us, complaining starts early. Hearing
the alarm clock ring in the morning sparks an
objection that we have to get up.

Now, if only the apostle Paul hadn't included the word *everything*. Doing *everything* without protest or dispute is hard. Some situations just call for complaining or arguing—I want to reserve the right under certain conditions.

Just think, though, what could happen in our relationships if we took this verse seriously. How peaceful our families would be if we didn't argue! Sit down with your family and show them this verse. See if you can get everyone to agree to practice it for one week. You may even make a rule that if anyone complains or argues, he or she has to put money in a fund to buy ice cream for the family at the end of the week. You may be surprised at the difference this verse will make!

30

The righteous will flourish like a palm tree, they will grow like a cedar of Lebanon; planted in the house of the LORD, they will flourish in the courts of our God. They will still bear fruit in old age, they will stay fresh and green.
PSALM 92:12–14

WHAT IS AHEAD

Have you noticed how fast birthdays seem to keep coming year after year after year? That means that, if we live long enough, each of us is going to grow old. I, for one, want to make the best of those golden years. I hope what Psalm 92 says about old age will be true in my life:

The righteous will flourish like a palm tree,
* they will grow like a cedar of Lebanon;*
* planted in the house of the LORD,*
* they will flourish in the courts of our God.*
They will still bear fruit in old age,
* they will stay fresh and green.*
PSALM 92:12–14

Stay fresh and green. Still bear fruit in old age. Now that's the way to live! Not worrying about wrinkles or aches and pains, but radiant with a desire to live life to its fullest.

We may be nearing old age but that shouldn't stop us from setting goals for the future. *The Message* paraphrase of Paul's words to the Philippians says, "Friends, don't get me wrong: By no means do I count myself an expert. . .but I've got my eye on the goal, where God is beckoning us onward—to Jesus. I'm off and running, and I'm not turning back" (Philippians 3:13–14).

High in the Swiss Alps a monument has been erected in honor of a mountain guide who died in the attempt to rescue a stranded tourist. The message inscribed on the stone reads, HE DIED CLIMBING. That's the motto I would like to leave behind when my time on earth ends. So, I'm off and running. I hope to still bear fruit in old age—and stay fresh and green.

31

Simon Peter answered him, "Lord, to whom shall we go? You have the words of eternal life."
JOHN 6:68

BAD THINGS HAPPEN

God could have prevented it—*why didn't He? He can change any circumstance I face.*

Do thoughts like these ever go through your mind? If you're honest, you'll have to admit they do. You don't like what God is allowing in your life. So what are your options?

You have two choices: either to turn away from God and become bitter, or to turn to God and rely on Him even though you don't understand why you're suffering.

It's pretty obvious that option 1—turning away from God and becoming bitter—is not a good choice. That leaves option 2—turning to God. When you choose to rely on God, you give up relying on any logical reason for what is happening. You simply say, "God, I am going to rely on You and no one else. I ask You to solve this problem. But if You don't, I will trust You anyway."

Like the three Israelites in the book of Daniel who were thrown into the fiery furnace, you say, "If we are thrown into the blazing furnace, the God we serve is able to deliver us from it. . .but even if he does not…we will not serve your gods" (Daniel 3:17–18). If you think they burned, read their story.

Let's say you decide you can't trust God. Whom will you trust? When some of the crowds turned back and no longer followed Jesus because they didn't like His teachings, He asked the disciples if they wanted to leave, too. Peter answered, "Lord, to whom shall we go? You have the words of eternal life" (John 6:68).

When disaster happens, to whom will *you* go?

32

*We remember before our God and Father
your work produced by faith, your labor
prompted by love, and your endurance
inspired by hope in our Lord Jesus Christ.*
1 THESSALONIANS 1:3

WHEN YOU NEED
REASONS TO KEEP GOING

At 5:30 a.m. our daughter Nancy called us for help. The family dog had quit breathing. Since her husband had to leave immediately for the airport, could my husband take the dog out of the house before their four children awoke? Fortunately, by the time he was dressed, the dog had revived. But the next morning brought another crisis: a woman drove directly into Nancy's brand-new car. The following day her daughter called from school with severe stomach pains. Could she please come pick her up? It was one of those weeks when Nancy felt like giving up.

The early Christians had reasons for giving

up. They faced suffering, persecution, and constant threats, yet they kept on. How?

In 1 Thessalonians 1:3, Paul speaks of three practical qualities Christians should have: faith, love, and hope. First, he says their work was produced by faith. That means they did what they did, believing that someday it would all make a difference. Caring for toddlers, going to work every day, making sacrifices for other people—they all have to be done by faith.

Next Paul talks about "labor prompted by love." I think of labor as any work that is super hard. What kept the early believers going was that Jesus had done so much for them; no sacrifice was too great if they would do it for Him.

The last quality is hope—the hope of heaven. Author Tim LaHaye says, "For the believer, this life is as bad as it gets!" But we can endure because we have a future with the Lord.

33

*"The eternal God is your refuge,
and underneath are the everlasting arms."*
DEUTERONOMY 33:27

UNDERNEATH ARE
THE EVERLASTING ARMS

When the airplane I'm in hits turbulence during a flight, I'm a candidate for the "Chicken of the Air" award. I just don't like being tossed around. But I've found a verse in the Bible that helps a lot: "The eternal God is your refuge, and underneath are the everlasting arms" (Deuteronomy 33:27). Picturing God's big arms underneath that bouncing plane calms my emotions. God's everlasting arms hold the plane as a loving father holds his newborn child.

Although air travel was several thousand years yet in the future when he wrote these words, David tells us that there is no place we can go that we will not find God already there. He writes, "If I go up to the heavens, you are there; if I make my bed in the depths, you are there. If I rise on the wings of the dawn, if I settle on the far side of the sea, even there your hand will guide me, your right hand will hold me fast" (Psalm 139:8–10).

Maybe it's not plane travel that makes you feel insecure. Maybe your job is shaky. Or you dread going to the doctor. Or your marriage is rocky.

Read these verses. David said, "Though an army besiege me, my heart will not fear; though war break out against me, even then will I be confident. . . . For in the day of trouble he will keep me safe in his dwelling; he will hide me in the shelter of his sacred tent and set me high upon a rock" (Psalm 27:3, 5).

Remember, God is our refuge, and we're in His everlasting arms!

34

For I am convinced that neither death nor life, neither angels nor demons, neither the present nor the future, nor any powers, neither height nor depth, nor anything else in all creation, will be able to separate us from the love of God that is in Christ Jesus our Lord.
ROMANS 8:38–39

HE LOVES ME

When writer Elizabeth Prentiss was a teenager in the 1800s, she became so disgusted with her temper and lack of self-control that she was sure God could never love her. She told a minister friend, "I can't be good two minutes at a time. I do everything I do not want to do and do nothing I try and pray to do."

The minister replied, half to himself, "Poor child. . . All you say may be true. I daresay it is. But God loves you. He loves you."

Then he told her, "Go home and say over and over to yourself, 'I am a wayward, foolish child. But He loves me! I have disobeyed and grieved Him ten thousand times. But He loves me! I have lost faith. . .I do not love Him; I am even angry with Him! But He loves me!' "

At home Elizabeth knelt down to pray. As she tells it, "All my wasted, childish, wicked life came and stared me in the face. I looked at it and said with tears of joy, 'But He loves me!' "

Absolutely nothing you can do will keep God from loving you. The apostle Paul wrote, "I am convinced that neither death nor life, neither angels nor demons, neither the present nor the future, nor any powers, neither height nor depth, nor anything else in all creation, will be able to separate us from the love of God that is in Christ Jesus our Lord" (Romans 8:38–39).

When you are tempted to despair at the long list of your shortcomings, no matter what you have done wrong, friend, don't forget to add, "But He loves me—unconditionally!"

35

One thing God has spoken, two things I have heard: "Power belongs to you, God, and with you, Lord, is unfailing love"; and, "You reward everyone according to what they have done."
Psalm 62:11–12

STRONG AND LOVING

When we think of masculine and feminine characteristics, we often think of strength as masculine and love as feminine. Of course, that's an oversimplification. But I find it interesting that the Bible says God has both of these traits. Psalm 62:11–12 says, "You, O God, are strong. . .you, O Lord, are loving."

If God were only strong, I might be afraid of Him. I'm well aware He could zap me into eternity in a split second. If He were only loving but not strong, He might not be able to help me. His love would reach out to me in compassion. He would feel sorry for me, but that's as far as it would go. Instead, He is the ideal Father—both strong and loving. He is loving enough to care and strong enough to help.

I'm encouraged when I read verses about God's strength like: "What god is there in heaven or on earth who can do the deeds and mighty works you do?" (Deuteronomy 3:24), and "Your arm is endowed with power; your hand is strong" (Psalm 89:13).

And I am comforted when I find verses that tell me that my strong God is also loving: "You are my strength, I watch for you; you, God, are my fortress, my God on whom I can rely" (Psalm 59:9–10).

A loving God who is strong! That's exactly what we need. Take a moment right now to acknowledge that He is strong enough to help you in the situation you face today. Then thank Him that He loves you and cares for you. As the psalmist said, "He is my loving God. . .and my deliverer" (Psalm 144:2).

36

"I know your deeds, that you are neither cold nor hot. I wish you were either one or the other!"

REVELATION 3:15

(THE WHOLE STORY: REVELATION 3:14–22)

A FAMOUS CHURCH

Of the many well-known churches in the world, one became famous for all the wrong reasons. The apostle John tells us about it in Revelation 3. It's the church of Laodicea, located in what is now Turkey.

God says about the people in this church: "I know your deeds, that you are neither cold nor hot. I wish you were either one or the other! So, because you are lukewarm—neither hot nor cold—I am about to spit you out of my mouth" (verses 15–16). Strong words!

The worst thing was that these people didn't realize how bad they were. Because they had money, they didn't think they needed anything else. The Bible says, "You do not realize that you are wretched, pitiful, poor, blind and naked" (verse 17).

Many Christians today are like the people of that church. Their relationship with God has grown distant. No longer do they enjoy a sense of God's presence or do the things that please God. Yet God doesn't give up on them. He stands at their hearts' door, knocking—"If anyone hears my voice and opens the door, I will come in and eat with that person, and they with me" (verse 20). Instead of rejecting them, He wants to nurture them by His presence. He offers them His companionship, knowing that the fire in their hearts will be rekindled by the warmth of His love.

If you have grown lukewarm in your relationship with God, open the door of your heart and invite Him in. Listen to His words in the Bible and share your deepest thoughts with Him in prayer. He's knocking on your heart's door right now.

37

*And my God will meet all your needs according
to the riches of his glory in Christ Jesus.*
PHILIPPIANS 4:19

POTATOES

The Great Depression hung over America
in the 1930s when my dad accepted the
pastorate of a small church with a weekly salary
of only $10—barely enough to buy groceries
and pay the rent.

One day, Mr. Smith, a farmer in the church,
backed his little white pickup truck into my
parents' yard and unloaded a hundred-pound
sack of potatoes, saying, "When these are gone
let me know and I'll bring you another sack."
My parents thanked him gratefully.

One hundred pounds of potatoes! They
felt like millionaires. You can do so many
different things with potatoes: boil them, bake
them, fry them, stuff them, and more. They
really enjoyed those potatoes.

But as the weeks went by, the number

of potatoes in the sack dwindled. My dad remembered Mr. Smith's offer to bring another sack. He said he didn't know whether it was pride or stubbornness, but he simply could not bring himself to ask Mr. Smith for more potatoes. But he did get down on his knees and ask God to tell Mr. Smith that they needed more potatoes.

Do you know in less than two weeks Mr. Smith unloaded another one-hundred-pound sack of potatoes? There were exactly two potatoes left in the original sack.

How amazing to think that they had a God who loved them so much that He would even keep track of the number of potatoes in their sack! God knew exactly how and when to meet my parents' needs. Take heart, He will meet your needs as well. As the apostle Paul said, "My God will meet all your needs according to the riches of his glory in Christ Jesus" (Philippians 4:19).

38

The fruit of the righteous is a tree of life,
and the one who is wise saves lives.
PROVERBS 11:30

THE JOB IS TOO SMALL

Several years ago the board of the Standard Oil Company was looking for a manager for their new office in China. He or she had to be able to speak Chinese fluently, be a qualified businessman, a born leader, and be under age thirty. After much deliberation, there was still no one who met the requirements.

Finally one of the board members spoke: "I do know a man who fits the qualifications. He is twenty-eight years old, he was valedictorian of his class, he is a born leader and speaks Chinese fluently, and lives in China."

The board was at once interested, and commissioned the member to go to China and offer the man the job. He was instructed to get him at any price.

After traveling halfway around the world,

the man presented the opportunity to his friend, offering him a comfortable salary. But his friend, a missionary, shook his head. "No." The man raised the amount several times, but each time the answer was no!

"What *will* you take?" the man asked.

The missionary replied, "Oh, there is nothing wrong with the salary. It is magnificent, but the job is too small. I have a small salary, but a big job. You offer me a big salary, but a little job. I would be foolish to stop winning people to the Lord and start selling oil."

Whether you are a missionary or a lay person, it is just as true today. In Proverbs 11 King Solomon, who was both wise and rich, wrote, "The one who is wise saves lives" (Proverbs 11:30). Winning souls to the Lord is the biggest job in the world.

39

*He saved us, not because of righteous things
we had done, but because of his mercy.*
TITUS 3:5

SAVED BY GOOD DEEDS
OR GOD'S MERCY?

My grandfather was the son of an Episcopalian minister. Though he was brought up in a strict environment, he had never truly had a relationship with Jesus Christ. In fact, Grandpa made up his mind that when he left home he was going to live it up. But when he did, he found no real satisfaction, so he returned to church. Being a traveling salesman, he joined the Gideons, that fine organization of Christian businessmen who place Bibles in hotel rooms around the world.

Grandpa made a trip to collect the annual donation of a Mr. Noble to the Gideons. After presenting his check to Grandpa, this elderly gentleman asked him, "Are you saved?" to which Grandpa replied, "I'm doing the best

I can, and I hope to get to heaven."

The white-haired gentleman said, "That's a sure ticket to hell for you. Tell me, what are you doing to get to heaven?" Grandpa said he was striving to live a good life, to be a good husband and father, and to be a respectable citizen.

The old gentleman snapped his fingers and said, "That won't count that much toward getting you to heaven." Then Mr. Noble told him that salvation did not depend on what *he* did, but what Jesus had done *for* him on the cross. Soon they were both on their knees, praying, and my grandfather finally surrendered his life to Christ.

The Bible says God saves us "not because of righteous things we [have] done, but because of his mercy" (Titus 3:5). We *all* qualify for that!

40

We love because he first loved us.
1 JOHN 4:19

LOVING OBEDIENCE

I attended a conference where one of the speakers asked an interesting question: "Which are you more afraid of—breaking God's commandments or breaking His heart?" That hit home with me. Most of us know that God wants us to do right and reject wrong.

But even beyond obedience, God wants an intimate relationship with us. There is such a need for us to obey God because we love Him, because we don't want to do anything that would bring heartache to our loving heavenly Father.

We need loving obedience in five areas of our lives: our mind, our will, our emotions, our body, and our time. Now, if you're alive and breathing, you struggle in one or more areas. I struggle with lovingly obeying God when it comes to taking care of my body. Exercise?

I don't want to do it. I also struggle with wanting to play when I should work. And most of all, I struggle when I need to confront someone about an issue and I don't want to.

A friend struggles with her mind and emotions. She has a fear of serious illness. She can convince herself that she has the symptoms of nearly every illness she hears about. My friend has to lovingly obey God by focusing on God's promises to care for her.

I challenge you to listen, to be sensitive to God's voice, and then lovingly obey Him—not because He's going to punish you if you don't, but because you love Him so much you don't want to break His heart. John said, "We love him, because he first loved us" (1 John 4:19 KJV). What motivation for us!

41

Jesus said to [Zacchaeus],
"Today salvation has come to this house."

LUKE 19:9

(THE WHOLE STORY: LUKE 19:1–10)

GOD SEEKS THE LOST

One day while swimming along the bottom of the ocean, a professional diver noticed an oyster with a piece of paper in its mouth. He opened the oyster and held the paper close to his goggles. To his surprise, he found it was a Gospel tract explaining how to become a Christian.

Amazed, the diver realized, *I cannot hold out against God any longer since He has gone to so much trouble to track me down.* At the bottom of the ocean he repented of his sins and placed His faith in Jesus Christ.

Zacchaeus was a tax collector who was short on morals and in stature. He was in Jericho when Jesus arrived, but couldn't see Him over the crowd so he ran ahead and climbed a tree. When Jesus reached the tree, He looked up saying, "Zacchaeus, come down immediately. I must stay at your house today."

The people began to mutter, "He has gone to be the guest of a sinner."

Zacchaeus said, "Look, Lord! Here and now I give half of my possessions to the poor, and if I have cheated anybody out of anything, I will pay back four times the amount."

Jesus said, "Today salvation has come to this house. . . . For the Son of Man came to seek and to save the lost" (Luke 19:1–10).

If God is speaking loud and clear to you today, don't you think it's time for you to respond? Whether you are at the bottom of the ocean or in a tree or driving your car to work, He's calling you.

42

I plead with Euodia and I plead with
Syntyche to be of the same mind in the Lord.
PHILIPPIANS 4:2

WOMEN WHO CAN'T GET ALONG

When they came to me, the two women were at a heated impasse. They were both Sunday school leaders in a large church. The dilemma was that one strongly believed hexagonal crayons were best for young children to use, while the other insisted that round crayons were the only way to go. As ridiculous as it sounds, neither woman would give in.

A similar thing happened to two women in the Bible. Paul wrote, "I plead with Euodia and I plead with Syntyche to be of the same mind in the Lord" (Philippians 4:2). Like the two Sunday school leaders, these women were both energetic workers for the Lord. Many had come to faith in Christ through their efforts. But some difference of opinion had grown into an impasse.

I hate to admit it, but I've observed that this problem happens more often among women than men. In a board meeting, for instance, two men can argue vehemently about an issue. But when the meeting is over, they can go out and play basketball together without holding on to hard feelings. When two women disagree, they don't even want to talk to each other, let alone have lunch.

Yes, it's possible to believe in Christ, work hard for His kingdom, and yet have strong disagreements with others who are committed to the same cause. But there is no excuse for remaining unreconciled.

Psalm 133:1 NLT says, "How wonderful and pleasant it is when brothers"—and I might add sisters—"live together in harmony!" Do you need to iron out your differences with someone today?

43

The LORD is good, a refuge in times of trouble.
He cares for those who trust in him.
NAHUM 1:7

A REFUGE IN TIMES OF TROUBLE

You're leaving on a trip abroad when you learn there is a travel warning posted for your destination. Upon arriving at the airport, a bomb scare empties the terminal. Metal detectors, dogs sniffing your luggage—like it or not, the world is an uncertain place.

As never before, we need to hold on to the assurance that God cares for those who trust in Him. It's not enough to know that this promise is in the Bible. You need to know it's in your heart—internalized and made your own.

The short Old Testament book of Nahum was written about the Middle Eastern city of Nineveh whose people were cruel and wicked. Through the prophet Nahum, God graphically warned the Ninevites that they would be destroyed.

Yet smack dab in the middle of all the bad news is one of the most beautiful promises in the Bible. It's in Nahum 1:7. "The LORD is good, a refuge in times of trouble. He cares for those who trust in him."

God is a good God. When you have a personal relationship with Him, you have a refuge in trouble—a haven, a sanctuary, a place of safety, a shelter. I love the image in Psalm 91 of God as a mother hen protecting her chicks: "He will cover you with his feathers, and under his wings you will find refuge" (Psalm 91:4).

We live in a scary world, but remember that you have a God who "cares for those who trust in him."

44

And so we will be with the Lord forever.
1 Thessalonians 4:17
(the whole story: 1 Thessalonians 4:13–18)

With the Lord

Everybody wants to go to heaven when they die. Or at least, they certainly don't want to go to hell! But have you ever thought that one day you might suddenly find yourself in heaven not knowing your way around? Common belief is that the apostle Peter will welcome us, but actually the Bible doesn't say so.

You don't have to worry about feeling lost when you die. The Bible says that because Jesus is our Savior, we will be with Him. Paul says that to be away from the body is to be at home with the Lord (2 Corinthians 5:8). There is no intermediary place, no time lapse in between.

Notice Paul doesn't say, "To be absent from the body is to be in heaven." He says something far more fantastic: When we die, we'll instantly be in Jesus' presence—with Him.

Paul also tells us what will happen if we are still alive when Jesus returns. He says that "God will bring with Jesus those who have fallen asleep in him" (1 Thessalonians 4:14). He continues, "After that, we who are still alive and are left will be caught up together with them in the clouds to meet the Lord in the air. And so we will be with the Lord forever" (1 Thessalonians 4:17).

Just think of it! The One who walked with you through your problems and to whom you have spoken countless times in prayer, the One who died for you, the One who loves you more than anyone else—you're really going to be with Him, at home with Jesus forever. Magnificent promise!

45

*"Father, I have sinned against
heaven and against you."*
LUKE 15:21
(THE WHOLE STORY: LUKE 15:11–24)

MATURE PRAYER

Jesus told a story about a son who said to
his father, "Give me my share of the estate,"
and the father did so. The son then set off and
squandered all his wealth. Reduced to taking
a job feeding pigs, he was so hungry that even
the pigs' slop looked good to him.

Eventually he came to his senses and said,
"How many of my father's hired men have
food to spare, and here I am starving! I will
go back to my father and say to him: 'Father,
I have sinned against heaven and against you.
I am no longer worthy to be called your son;
make me like one of your hired men.' " So off
he went.

But while he was still a long way off, his
father ran to him and threw his arms around

him. The father told the servants, "Bring the best robe and put it on him. Put a ring on his finger and sandals on his feet. Let's have a feast and celebrate. For this son of mine was dead and is alive again; he was lost and is found" (Luke 15:12–24, excerpted).

Beyond this story of forgiveness and restoration is a lesson on prayer. The young son started out saying, "Father, give me my share of the estate." But his request changed to: "Father, make me like one of your hired men." Immature prayer stops with "Father, give me"—the long list of everything we want from God. Mature prayer goes on to say, "Father, make me—exactly what You want me to be."

After you've brought all your "give-me" requests to God, don't forget the "make-me" part.

46

Do not be anxious about anything, but in every situation, by prayer and petition, with thanksgiving, present your requests to God.
PHILIPPIANS 4:6

ANYTHING AND EVERYTHING

I'll give you a verse in the Bible that covers anything and everything that will happen to you today. You'll find it in Philippians 4:6. The first part says, "Don't worry about anything" (NLT). Now, that sounds simple to do—but only until something major strikes at the center of what you care most about. It could be the business you just started, or much more serious, your mate or one of your children. Then you find yourself thinking about the problem nonstop.

How can God tell you not to worry about anything when what you really care most about is falling apart? Well, the verse doesn't stop there. God goes on to say, "Instead, pray about everything." Prayer is the antidote God gives for worry. The big question is, have you tried it? Today, every time that worry pops in your mind, immediately turn it into a prayer for God's help. Our human tendency is to think that our worry is either too small to bother God about or too big for us to expect Him to fix. But nothing is too large or too small for God. That's why He tells us to pray about *everything*—yes, every worry that comes to mind.

The biggest problem most of us have with prayer is giving up too soon. We think that once we have prayed about a problem, that should take care of it. But it doesn't work that way. Remember, we need to pray every time we worry—and that can be pretty often on any day. God urges us to turn every worried thought into a prayer.

47

*Noah and his sons and his wife
and his sons' wives entered the ark
to escape the waters of the flood.*
GENESIS 7:7

(THE WHOLE STORY: GENESIS 6:1–8:18)

MRS. NOAH

All the people of the world trace their lineage to this woman. She lived during a period when morals sank to an all-time low and the earth was filled with violence.

She is not Eve but her descendant, and lived at least ten generations after her. Her husband is mentioned over fifty times in the Bible. "Noah was a righteous man, blameless among the people of his time, and he walked faithfully with God" (Genesis 6:9). But she is only identified as "the wife of Noah."

When God told Noah He was going to destroy the world by a flood, the peoples of the earth had never even seen rain. For 120 years Noah warned of God's coming judgment, but no one listened. Can you imagine how hard it must have been for Mrs. Noah when people made fun of her husband, how she had to encourage him when he got tired of preaching with no results? Realize, too, her boys had no "good" kids to play with. Yet she must have raised her kids to be godly, because when the world was destroyed, God saved her three sons.

Life on the ark? Imagine living in a floating zoo with the windows closed for forty days and nights of rain. And they had to wait inside the ark for 150 more days before they could step out on dry land and begin a new life.

Mrs. Noah surely exemplified 1 Corinthians 15:58: "Let nothing move you. Always give yourselves fully to the work of the Lord, because you know that your labor in the Lord is not in vain." You, Mrs. Noah, belong in the Faith Hall of Fame.

48

"When the people willingly
offer themselves—praise the LORD!"
JUDGES 5:2
(THE WHOLE STORY: JUDGES 5:1–9)

VOLUNTEERS

Every organization that touches people's lives depends on a select group to help make it happen: the volunteers. Organizations also have paid staff, but they would never be able to accomplish what they do if it were not for hardworking, selfless volunteers who stuff envelopes, make repairs, count donations, and do anything that needs to be done. I know, because I've seen them at work in our own organization, Guidelines International Ministries.

In the Bible I found two verses about volunteers, and both times, the author was prompted to say, "Praise the Lord!" for them. Barak and Deborah were leading an important battle against Sisera, a Canaanite king who had cruelly oppressed Israel for twenty years. The leaders couldn't win the battle alone—volunteers made the difference that led them to victory.

After the battle, the leaders sang a song declaring, "When the princes in Israel take the lead, when the people willingly offer themselves—praise the LORD!" (Judges 5:2). I think the leader of any organization would heartily agree with that sentiment. When people offer to help, the battle can be won! In another part of the song, the leaders exclaimed, "My heart is with Israel's princes, with the willing volunteers among the people. Praise the LORD!" (Judges 5:9).

If you volunteer your time to make a difference in the lives of people, I want to say, "Thank you" to you today. Everything you do may be behind the scenes. But one day God will acknowledge what you have done, and then we will all say, "Praise the Lord!"

49

When your words came, I ate them;
they were my joy and my heart's delight,
for I bear your name, LORD God Almighty.
JEREMIAH 15:16

SPIRITUAL SURVIVAL

The flight attendant recited the instructions as the plane was taking off. "If loss of cabin pressure occurs, oxygen masks will drop. If you are traveling with a child, secure your own mask before putting the mask on your child." If you black out, you would not be able to help your child. It makes sense.

Yet when it comes to parenting, we mothers usually feel we must always tend to our children's needs before our own. Sometimes we're pretty close to blacking out from exhaustion.

Moms often come up short in availing themselves of spiritual resources. When I was mothering three young children, I wondered if it were possible to have a deep spiritual life.

There simply was no time for extensive Bible study or long periods of prayer. The best I could do was grab a few verses on the run and send up prayers of desperation, saying, "Lord, help me!"

So my advice to moms is, don't panic when a few days go by when you can't complete a Bible study and your prayers are very short. Consider a psalm as you brew the coffee, a prayer of praise as you look into your baby's face during a diaper change, or uplifting words from scripture tapes or CDs as you drive.

The same principle is true if you're responsible for the employees of a large corporation. You can't go very long without spiritual nourishment. The prophet Jeremiah said, "When your words came, I ate them; they were my joy and my heart's delight" (Jeremiah 15:16).

Make sure you keep spiritually "nibbling" daily when a "sit-down dinner" isn't possible!

50

And over all these virtues put on love, which
binds them all together in perfect unity.
Colossians 3:14

GOD'S WARDROBE

In Colossians 3 we're told to clothe ourselves
with seven characteristics. If we do, we'll
have an entire outfit—and all of the highest
quality!

The first on the list is *compassion*. That's
the shirt because it's worn close to the heart.
When our hearts are filled with compassion,
we'll reach out to others.

The second is *kindness*. Since it's our legs
that carry us to do helpful things for others,
kindness must be the skirt or pants.

The belt that secures kindness in place
is *patience*! With patience, we have the grace
to continue to treat others kindly even when
they're unresponsive.

Humility certainly must be the shoes, the
items closest to the ground. Shoes of humility

will take us to help those who are less fortunate than us.

For accessories, try *gentleness*. It's not very flashy, but oh so attractive. Peter says, "Your beauty should not come from outward adornment. . . . Rather, it should be that of. . .a gentle and quiet spirit, which is of great worth in God's sight" (1 Peter 3:3–4).

Item number six is *forgiveness*. This is the hat because forgiveness is first a decision you make in your head, then an emotion of the heart.

How about a coat to keep out the cold? Scripture says, "Over all these virtues put on love, which binds them all together in perfect unity" (Colossians 3:14). *Love* absolutely radiates warmth.

Don't you agree that the person wearing compassion, kindness, humility, gentleness, patience, forgiveness, and love is well dressed for any occasion? Let's wear God's wardrobe!

51

*In everything he [Amaziah] followed
the example of his father Joash.*
2 KINGS 14:3
(THE WHOLE STORY: 2 KINGS 14:1–4)

———————

THE POWER OF EXAMPLE

S teve Maxwell, a leader in the home school
movement, tells of a lesson he learned from
his son.

While moving his family to a new home,
they stopped at a restaurant to eat. When the
waiter took their order, Nathan, their eldest
son, spoke up. He told the waiter that they
would be asking the Lord to bless their food
and asked if there was anything they might
pray about for him. The waiter was taken
aback. Recovering, he said that his girlfriend's
father was in the hospital with a serious heart
problem, and they would appreciate prayer
for him. After the prayer, the waiter was clearly
moved and grateful.

Steve told his son Nathan how thankful he

was for his example, and that he was looking forward to asking others this same question in the future. Nathan explained that he had been with someone else who had done this, and he decided he would do it himself. Someone had set an example for Nathan, and Nathan learned from the example he saw.

The power of example! It is passed from person to person. Whether you realize it or not, you are mentoring people by your life. Some of the finest teaching is done not with words but by example.

You may never have heard of kings by the name of Amaziah and Joash, but we can learn something from them. Scripture says Amaziah "did what was right in the eyes of the LORD. . . . In everything he followed the example of his father Joash" (2 Kings 14:3). So Joash set the example, and his son Amaziah followed in his footsteps.

Be encouraged—people do notice what you do. Your example has the power to shape their lives.

52

*"Your Father knows what
you need before you ask him."*
MATTHEW 6:8

GOD IS A GREAT ACCOUNTANT

My dad, who was in ministry for seventy-four years, began preaching during the difficult days of the 1930s, when money was hard to come by.

Dad told that one day he had to mail an important letter. It had to be posted that day, but he did not have three cents to buy the needed stamp.

When the mailman came that very morning Dad received a letter from a friend and there, between the pages of the letter, was a three-cent stamp. No mention of the stamp was made in the letter, but the Lord had known, several days before, that he was going to need a postage stamp. The Lord had graciously put it into the heart of this friend to drop a stamp into the envelope.

Dad also remembered a time when he needed ten cents for something important— just ten cents, but he did not have it. Again a letter came with a dime thrown in. He used to exclaim, "How wonderful the Lord is to His children!"

I'm glad he told us these experiences, because it taught me that God is a great accountant. He knows exactly how much you have and how much you need at any given moment. The Bible says, "Your Father knows what you need before you ask him" (Matthew 6:8). And if God has supplied His children's needs in the past, you can be sure that He will also meet their present needs.

You may think, *God answers prayer for other people, but I don't know if He will for me.* Just try Him. For He knows what you need even before you ask Him.

53

*Indeed, we felt we had received the sentence of
death. But this happened that we might not rely
on ourselves but on God, who raises the dead.*

2 CORINTHIANS 1:9

THREE REASONS
WHY THIS HAPPENED

When you're deeply hurting, the question
that immediately comes to mind is:
Why? Why did this happen to me? Three
examples in the Bible give us three answers to
this troubling question.

The first is that pain comes because of
sin. Jeremiah 13:22 says, "And if you ask
yourself, 'Why has this happened to me?'—it
is because of your many sins." We may see this
connection in others but sometimes we're not
so quick to see this truth in ourselves.

Another reason God allows pain is so that
He will be praised. Does that seem strange
to you? Just before Jesus healed a blind man,
the religious leaders asked whose sin had

caused the blindness. Jesus answered, "Neither this man nor his parents sinned. . .but this happened so that the works of God might be displayed in him" (John 9:3). God may want you to be a showcase of His supernatural power so that people will acknowledge Him.

Third, Paul said that painful experiences happen to us "that we might not rely on ourselves but on God" (2 Corinthians 1:9). We quickly realize, *I can't fix this! I really need God's help!* There's nothing like an impossible situation to make us realize how helpless we are.

If right now you are dealing with a painful problem, God may be saying, "There's sin here that we need to talk about." Or maybe He's going to send such a miraculous solution that all you can say is, "Praise Him!" Or maybe He's helping you realize how totally dependent you are on Him and how totally dependable He is. Just listen!

54

A young girl from Israel. . .served Naaman's wife. She said to her mistress, "If only my master would see the prophet who is in Samaria! He would cure him of his leprosy."

2 KINGS 5:2–3

(THE WHOLE STORY: 2 KINGS 5:1–15)

WHERE'S THE PICCOLO?

The famous conductor Sir Michael Costa was leading an orchestra rehearsal with hundreds of instruments and voices. The choir sang at full voice, accompanied by the thundering of the organ, the rolling of drums, and the blaring of horns.

In the midst of the music, the piccolo player, far up in a corner, said to himself, "It doesn't matter what I do," and he stopped playing. Suddenly, the great conductor flung up his hands and brought the rehearsal to a complete standstill. "Where is the piccolo?!" he cried. His sharp ear had noticed its absence. And so for him the whole piece had been spoiled.[1]

What about you? In life's orchestra, have you ever felt like the piccolo player—insignificant and hidden?

The Bible tells the story of how a simple servant played an important role in the life of a highly-regarded man. Naaman was commander of the army of the king of Aram. Then he contracted leprosy.

His armies had taken a young Israeli girl captive, and she became a servant to Naaman's wife. She was definitely "just" a piccolo player—a prisoner, a slave. But she spoke up and said to her mistress, "If only my master would see the prophet [Elisha] who is in Samaria! He would cure him of his leprosy" (2 Kings 5:3). Naaman did just that. Through Elisha, God healed Naaman of the disease. From that point on, Naaman said he would worship only the true God. God used a simple captive maid to draw an important man to Himself.

You make a difference in this life. Keep playing your piccolo. The Divine Conductor of life's orchestra is listening for your part.

[1]Corrie ten Boom, *Not I But Christ* (Nashville, TN: Thomas Nelson Publishers, 1984), 135.

55

*Then they cried to the Lord in their trouble,
and he saved them from their distress. He
brought them out of darkness, the utter
darkness, and broke away their chains.*
Psalm 107:13–14

No Pit Too Deep

By her own admission, she was a prostitute, a lesbian, an alcoholic, and a stripper. Only twenty-four years old and in prison for a year now on a murder charge, she was also a single mom with two kids.

She wrote me from prison to tell me that four months previously, Jesus had given her a new life. When she thought she was "finished," God rescued her, and now, she writes, "I am so happy to be alive in Jesus Christ."

While she was in prison, someone sent her my book *Created for a Purpose*. She read it and then wrote to say that she now knows God has a unique purpose for her life. My eyes filled with tears of joy when I read her letter. What a miracle God has done in her life!

This young woman is a glowing example of Psalm 107:13–14: "Then they cried to the LORD in their trouble, and he saved them from their distress. He brought them out of darkness, the utter darkness, and broke away their chains."

Maybe you, too, are chained in a pit. You're feeling that you've wasted your days— that you've gone too far for even God to restore your life. Dear friend, that simply is *not* true. Corrie ten Boom, a Dutch Christian who survived the horrors of the Ravensbrück concentration camp in World War 2, said, "There is no pit so deep that God's love is not deeper still." God can change your life; turn to Him with all your heart.

56

*It was good for me to be afflicted
so that I might learn your decrees.*
PSALM 119:71
(THE WHOLE STORY: PSALM 119:67–71)

GETTING MY ATTENTION

Her name was Carol, and she was in her eighties. The thing that impressed me most about her was the sweet attention she devoted to the Lord. Every morning during her quiet time with God, after she read some scripture, she would write a letter to Him. In these letters she would thank God for His goodness to her and ask Him for her needs. She would also tell Him about the circumstances that she didn't like. Each letter was Carol's prayer to the Lord, and this practice prepared her to face each day.

Carol was a volunteer at our Guidelines Ministries office for almost twenty years. So many times when she was going through difficult circumstances, I've heard her say something like: "The Lord is so good. If necessary, He wakes me up at two o'clock in the morning to talk to me. He loves me too much to let me go my own way. So if I know what's good for me, I'll listen to Him and learn what He wants to teach me, so He doesn't have to keep trying to get my attention."

Yes, God has interesting ways of getting our attention. Sometimes He speaks softly in our hearts. Other times He stops us in our tracks with a roadblock so big, we have no choice but to turn to Him. Either way, His motivation is love.

The writer of Psalm 119 said, "It was good for me to be afflicted so that I might learn your decrees" (verse 71). Thanks, Carol, for being a living example of that truth.

57

Therefore encourage one another and build
each other up, just as in fact you are doing.
1 THESSALONIANS 5:11

TEN THINGS I LOVE ABOUT YOU

When birthdays or Christmas roll around, do you ever wonder what to give that special person in your life who seems to have everything? My friend Angie suggests an album or scrapbook or a card entitled "Ten Things I Love about You." Although this gift will not cost you much money, it will require time for reflection as you go through the memories of your relationship and choose ten things that are special about that person.

This beautiful gift of "Ten Things I Love about You" can be given to your eight-year-old son or your ninety-year-old grandma—it fits all sizes and ages perfectly.

It's strange, but we presume that those we care about already know their strengths and lovable qualities. But that's not necessarily true. Sometimes those closest to us have struggled in certain areas and don't realize how successful they have become in conquering their difficulties. Instead of obstacles, those areas of their lives are now blessings—and they need you to tell them.

The Bible says, "Encourage one another and build each other up" (1 Thessalonians 5:11). Each of us would benefit from this kind of encouragement, and that's why this gift is so special.

Another plus is that whenever the recipient of your gift hurts you or needs your forgiveness—as eventually happens in every relationship—thinking of the ten things you love about that person will help your anger fade.

Take time to encourage that special person with a priceless gift that no one else can give. Both of you will be blessed.

58

"There is no one like the God of Jeshurun,
who rides across the heavens to help
you and on the clouds in his majesty."
DEUTERONOMY 33:26

SUPERMAN

Superman began as a comic-book character in June 1938. He grew in popularity, appearing in comic books, radio programs, newspaper comic strips, graphic novels, TV programs, movies, and even a Broadway musical. Wearing his familiar costume of red, blue, and yellow with the stylized "S," he has been a hero figure to millions.

In some versions of the story, his arrival on earth hints of a similarity to the birth of Jesus. In the movie version, Superman's father, played by Marlon Brando, tells his son to lead ordinary men to righteousness, saying, "For this reason above all—their capacity for good—I have sent them to you, my only son."

There is certainly a hunger in the human

heart for somebody bigger than we are. We want someone to look up to, someone who can accomplish incredible feats that we cannot, someone to fight the evil forces we see furiously at work in the world.

Fortunately, we have Someone who can do exactly those things. The Lord God Almighty is His name. "There is no one like the God of Jeshurun, who rides across the heavens to help you and on the clouds in his majesty" (Deuteronomy 33:26). And who was Jeshurun? Scholars tell us it was a poetic name for the people of Israel, used to express affection. It means "the dear upright people" (see Deuteronomy 32:15, 33:5, 26; Isaiah 44:2).

Superman can't be everywhere at once, and there are feats that Superman can't do, but "Nothing is impossible with God" (Luke 1:37 NLT). He is the real superhero. Aren't you glad you know Him?

59

Jesus answered. . . "What is that to you?
You must follow me."
JOHN 21:22
(THE WHOLE STORY: JOHN 21:1–25)

WHAT IS THAT TO YOU? FOLLOW ME!

I love the story of the conversation between
Simon Peter and Jesus on the shores of the
Sea of Galilee after Jesus rose from the dead.

Peter and Jesus had some unfinished
business. Remember what happened? Peter
had denied Jesus three times before Jesus was
crucified. But now Jesus turns to Peter and
asks, "Simon, do you love Me?" Peter answers,
"Yes, Lord, You know that I love You." Jesus
asks the question three times. Three denials
and three professions of love. Then Jesus tells
Peter ahead of time that when he is old he will
glorify God by being executed—tradition says
by crucifixion. Jesus then adds a command,
"Follow Me!" (John 21:19).

You can always count on Peter to ask the

questions you would have liked to ask if you had the nerve. Peter sees his fellow disciple John, and asks, "Lord, what about him?" (John 21:21). Don't you love his audacity? It's as if he is saying, "Lord, is he going to have to suffer as much as I?" In our day we compare ourselves with other Christians and ask, "Why do I have more problems than she has?"

Jesus answers, "If I want him to remain alive until I return, what is that to you? You must follow me" (John 21:22).

Jesus would say the same thing to us today: "Don't compare My work in your life with the way I work in the lives of others." Your experience with God is made specifically for you. Our job is simply to follow the Lord wherever He leads us. Thank God for His custom-designed plan for you! Just obey Him one day or even one hour, at a time. Who knows how He will use your life to bless others!

60

"His master replied, 'Well done, good and faithful servant! You have been faithful with a few things; I will put you in charge of many things. Come and share your master's happiness!' "

MATTHEW 25:21

FLORENCE NIGHTINGALE

Florence Nightingale, the founder of modern nursing, was born in 1820 to a wealthy English family.

When Florence was seventeen, she heard God call her for a special purpose in life. That calling was to help the sick and poor by becoming a nurse—in those days a lowly position that was considered to be "working class."

When England entered the Crimean War, Florence and a team of thirty-eight nurses went to Turkey and later Crimea to help the wounded soldiers. The military hospitals were filthy, infested with rats and fleas that brought typhus and cholera. Florence herself contracted Crimean Fever. She made improvements, however, that helped bring the death rate down from 40 percent to 2 percent. Her work there was the inspiration for the founding of the International Red Cross.

Returning to England after the war, Florence campaigned for improving hospitals so that they would become places where lives were saved, not lost. Three years before she died, she received the Order of Merit, making her the first woman ever to receive it.

Florence wrote,

My life. . .show[ed] how a woman of very ordinary ability has been led by God in strange and unaccustomed paths to do in his service what he has done in her. And if I could tell you all, you would see how God has done all, and I nothing. I have worked hard, very hard, that is all; and I have never refused God anything.[1]

The Lord must have surely told her, "Well done, good and faithful servant!" (Matthew 25:21). Think about the circumstances God has placed you in. What can you do in His service to show all that He has done in you?

[1]Killy John and Alie Stibbe, *Bursting at the Seams* (Oxford, UK and Grand Rapids, MI: Monarch Books, 2004), 12.

61

Therefore, I urge you, brothers and sisters, in view of God's mercy, to offer your bodies as a living sacrifice, holy and pleasing to God—this is your true and proper worship. Do not conform to the pattern of this world, but be transformed by the renewing of your mind. Then you will be able to test and approve what God's will is—his good, pleasing and perfect will.

ROMANS 12:1–2

LIVING SACRIFICES

It was one of those days when I felt pressured by too much to do, and I was working hard to complete each task. Just then my husband asked me if I had time to run an errand for him. Something flared up inside me, and in my mind I immediately answered him with a very firm no. My answer wasn't audible, but I'm sure by the look on my face he detected that I didn't want to do what he asked.

As I quickly thought it over, I realized that I was the logical person to run the errand. After all, I had more time than he did. So I said, yes, and started for the car.

But inside I was still resentful of being interrupted. I climbed in the driver's seat, and as I started the car, I turned on the radio. Immediately I heard the words, "Have you ever presented your body to the Lord as a living sacrifice?" *Okay, Lord,* I thought. *I hear You.*

In Romans 12:1 Paul says, "Therefore, I urge you, brothers and sisters, in view of God's mercy, to offer your bodies as a living sacrifice, holy and pleasing to God." Yes, I had made that commitment. But doing it in a beautiful, candlelit service is one thing; living out that commitment in everyday life is another. I confessed my lack of willingness and asked His forgiveness.

You, too, at one time or another may have offered your life to the Lord as a living sacrifice. But maybe you, like me, need to go back to the altar from time to time and do it again.

62

*To this you were called, because Christ
suffered for you, leaving you an example,
that you should follow in his steps.*

1 PETER 2:21

THE POWER OF TOUCH

Missionary doctor Paul Brand is famous
for his contributions to stopping leprosy
in poor areas of the world. Dr. Brand worked
with lepers who had been ostracized by their
communities, for the disease had long been
incorrectly thought to be contagious.

Dr. Brand tells that one day in India he
was examining the hands of a man, trying to
explain to him that he could halt the progress
of the leprosy, and perhaps restore some
movement. But he could do little about the
man's facial deformities. Dr. Brand joked
with him a bit, laying his hand on the man's
shoulder. "Your face is not so bad," he said
with a wink, "and it shouldn't get any worse
if you take the medication. After all, we men

don't have to worry so much about our faces. It's the women who fret over every bump and wrinkle." He expected the man to smile, but instead he began to shake with muffled sobs.

"Have I done something wrong?" Dr. Brand asked his assistant in English. "No, doctor," said the nurse. "He says he is crying because you put your hand around his shoulder. Until he came here no one had touched him for many years."[1]

Jesus touched people—the blind, the disabled, and yes, even people with leprosy—giving us an example that we "should follow in his steps" (1 Peter 2:21).

Sometimes we just don't realize how much someone needs our touch. Of course, it should be appropriate—the right person at the right time in the right way. See if there is someone in your life who needs this loving encouragement today.

[1]Dr. Paul Brand and Philip Yancey, *The Gift of Pain* (Manila, Philippines: OMF Literature Inc., 2000), 106.

63

Let the peace of Christ rule in your
hearts, since as members of one body you
were called to peace. And be thankful.
COLOSSIANS 3:15

LET THE PEACE OF GOD RULE— AND BE THANKFUL

Two of my grandchildren, ages six and nine at the time, were fighting. Heated words flew back and forth. Finally I interrupted them. "Carson, tell me one thing you like about Ryan—just one." It took awhile before he could think of anything, but finally he admitted, "Well, he helps me Rollerblade."

I can't remember now if Ryan, in turn, came up with anything or not, but they did quit arguing. It's almost impossible to stay angry with someone when you're thinking about one thing you like about that person.

The apostle Paul must have known that when he wrote to the Colossians, "Let the peace of Christ rule in your hearts, since as members of one body you were called to peace. And be thankful" (Colossians 3:15).

Anger and thankfulness are almost mutually exclusive. You can't be angry with someone and thankful for that person at the same time. Paul was saying, "Let the peace of Christ be the umpire in your disputes."

When we think of peace, we often think of an image like a perfectly calm lake. But preacher G. Campbell Morgan said that the word for peace used in the Bible is "not a stillness in which there is no movement at all . . . . It is the ending of strife and conflict."[1] It's that blessed relief that comes when the conflict is over.

That person you're angry with right now—isn't there one thing that you're thankful for about him? You may have to think very hard to come up with something. But if you do, your anger will begin to subside. Try it!

---

[1]G. Campbell Morgan, *The Corinthian Letters of Paul* (Westwood, NJ: Fleming H. Revell Company, 1946), 15.

64

He appointed twelve that they might be with him and that he might send them out to preach.
MARK 3:14

OH, HOW I'LL LOVE YOU!

Richard Abanes wrote a beautiful love song meant to be sung at weddings. The refrain goes,

And I'll honor you, I'll comfort you,
abide with you forever.
I'll be true to you, stay near to you,
forsake you never.
I will laugh with you, I will cry with you,
We will walk through life together;
And I'll love you, oh, how I'll love you.[1]

What bride wouldn't want to hear her groom pledge his love so beautifully? I couldn't help thinking that this is also the kind of relationship God wants with each of us. God has demonstrated that He desires a bond with us. Why else does God call Himself our Father? Why else is the Body of Christ, made up of all believers, pictured as the bride of Christ?

When Jesus called the disciples, "He appointed twelve. . .that they might be with him" (Mark 3:14). Oh yes, after that He sent them out to preach. But first, He called them to be with Him. That's how we get to know the Lord—by being with Him.

Two men in the Bible, we're told, walked with God—Enoch and Noah (Genesis 5:22, 24; 6:9). No wonder they knew Him so well. If we just spend time walking and talking with God, we, too, will grow to be more like Him.

Here's another thought. My husband knows beyond the shadow of a doubt that I love him. But he still wants to hear me tell him so every day—and so does God. Sit quietly for a moment and tell Him today.

[1]"Oh, How I'll Love You," music and lyrics by Richard Abanes © 1998. Used by permission.

65

*My guilt has overwhelmed me
like a burden too heavy to bear.*
Psalm 38:4

God's Hook

When she entered college, Pamela's relationship with her mom started to become strained, and from that point on things only grew worse. She remembers, "We just kept trying to be close, only to hurt each other again and again."[1] Both mother and daughter genuinely wanted to restore the broken relationship. So they decided to take a car trip together to patch things up.

The tension was pretty bad at first, but while they were in a restaurant Pamela finally poured out her heart about the things for which she needed forgiveness. To her surprise, her mother responded, "Sweetheart, I forgave you for all of those things years ago. You just didn't take them off of your hook and put them on God's."[2]

I love that word picture—taking your sins off your hook and putting them on God's! Sometimes we ask God to forgive our failures, but then we continue to carry guilt for them. Like David, we could say, "My guilt has overwhelmed me like a burden too heavy to bear" (Psalm 38:4). But God never intended it that way. Jesus said, "Come to me, all you who are weary and burdened, and I will give you rest" (Matthew 11:28). God is ready to carry your burdens for you, even the burden of guilt.

When I was a kid, I remember a wall plaque that said, "Let go and let God." Could this be the day that you would do just that? Right now let go of your failure and let God take care of it. Accept His forgiveness. Take your load off of your hook and put it on God's!

[1]Pamela Sonnenmoser, "Road Trip to Forgiveness" in *The Gift of Letting Go: Powerful Stories of Forgiveness* (Colorado: Honor Books, 2005), 204.
[2]Ibid., 205.

66

*What, then, shall we say in response to these
things? If God is for us, who can be against
us? He who did not spare his own Son, but gave
him up for us all—how will he not also, along
with him, graciously give us all things?*
ROMANS 8:31–32

TEN WAYS TO REDUCE STRESS

A friend recently sent me a list of "Thirty-Six Ways Christians Can Reduce Stress." No, I won't list all thirty-six, but let me share just ten ideas with you.

1. *Get up on time so you can start the day unrushed.* Let me add that it would be great if, before you tackle your responsibilities, you include time for Bible reading and prayer.

2. *Simplify and unclutter the rest of your day.* Allow more time than you think you need to do things and to get to places.

3. *Take one day at a time, separating*

worries from concerns. If the situation is a concern, ask God what to do about it. If it's a worry, turn it over to Him and forget it.

4. *Delegate tasks to others who are more capable.* It's an ego-trip to think you're the only one who can do the job.

5. *Carry a Bible with you to read while waiting in line.* That's a great way to use time. Another good use of time is to listen to an inspirational CD or MP3 while driving.

6. Having problems? *Talk to God on the spot.*

7. *Keep on hand a folder of favorite scripture verses or encouraging quotations.* You can also write them on cards you can carry with you.

8. *Be kind to unkind people*—they probably need kindness the most.

9. *Remind yourself that you are not the general manager of the universe.* God is quite capable of taking care of what you can't.

10. Every night before going to sleep, *think of one thing you're grateful for that you've never thanked God for before.* You'll sleep well.

67

Praise be to the God and Father of our Lord Jesus Christ, the Father of compassion and the God of all comfort, who comforts us in all our troubles, so that we can comfort those in any trouble with the comfort we ourselves receive from God.

2 Corinthians 1:3–4

GALS

Fifty ladies attended the luncheon that day. They all had something in common. Each of them has experienced how it is to wake up one morning and realize she is starting a new chapter in her life—as a widow.

Most married women will know how it is to live without husbands. Currently three-fourths of the people who are living at age seventy-five are women.

These women inspire me. They call themselves GALS ("Get a Life, Sister"). I see them using their gifts, time, and resources to bless others. Some have a ministry of prayer. Some minister to the elderly. Many are using their influence to impact their grandchildren. Each lives with precious memories, not "getting over" grief but getting on with living a life of meaning.

My friend Dee Green is such a person. For many years she worked alongside her husband, Paul, in ministry. Then with little warning, Paul went to be with the Lord. At first Dee didn't even want to live. But then God spoke to her heart and reassured her that He had a plan and unique work for her to do.

Many times I've called on Dee for help when a friend of mine has lost her husband. Dee knows how to rejoice with those who rejoice and weep with those who weep. She herself knows well the One the apostle Paul calls "the God of all comfort, who comforts us in all our troubles, so that we can comfort those in any trouble with the comfort we ourselves have receive from God" (2 Corinthians 1:3–4). Thanks, Dee, for modeling how to reach out to others who are in need.

68

*The LORD said, "I have indeed
seen the misery of my people."*

EXODUS 3:7

(THE WHOLE STORY: EXODUS 3:7–8)

———————————

GOD IS CONCERNED ABOUT YOU

Are you going through a time when
you're feeling down—below sea level—
struggling just to stay alive in the middle of
your problems? I wish I could change your
circumstances, but I can't. But I do have some
words from the Bible to encourage you.

First, here's what I want you to do. Think
back to the time when God's people, the
Israelites, were slaves in Egypt. Just think of
how life was for them as they suffered under
the tyranny of the Pharaohs. Maybe there are
some parallels between their troubles and what
you are going through.

For instance, you're stuck in this
impossible situation where you don't see any
way out, right? That's how the Israelites felt.

When they cried out to God, nothing seemed to happen.

But then something *did* happen. God intervened. And everything changed fast. "The LORD said, '*I have indeed seen* the misery of my people. . . *I have heard* them crying out. . .and *I am concerned* about their suffering. So *I have come down to rescue* them'" (Exodus 3:7–8, italics added).

Dear friend, God has not forgotten you. As He told His people so long ago, He does see you, He hears you, He is concerned, and He will rescue you. Cast your load of cares on the Lord and see if He doesn't bring you into a place of blessing in your life.

God says, "Remember. . .I have made you, you are my servant. . .I will not forget you" (Isaiah 44:21).

69

*And whatever you do, whether in word or deed,
do it all in the name of the Lord Jesus, giving
thanks to God the Father through him.*
COLOSSIANS 3:17

SMALL OBEDIENCES

As a woman, every day you do so many *little* things, don't you? You see to it that dirty clothes are laundered, groceries are bought, meals are prepared, dental appointments are made, homework is done. The list goes on and on. A woman's life is made up of seemingly endless little things to do.

But little things are important. Evangelist F. B. Meyer said,

*Do not try to do a great thing; you may
waste all your time waiting for the opportunity which may never come. But since little
things are always claiming your attention,
do them. . .for the glory of God.*

Meyer echoes what the apostle Paul wrote in Colossians 3:17: "And whatever you do, whether in word or deed, do it all in the name of the Lord Jesus, giving thanks to God the Father through him."

I like to think of little things as "small obediences." Cardinal John Henry Newman said that taking up the cross of Christ consists of the continual practice of small duties that may be distasteful to us.

When I was caring for my young children, one of them was always needing Mom—not for anything "important"—just to settle an argument or mop up a spill, while the phone was ringing and the pasta was boiling over on the stove. I had little time to do anything "spiritual," such as long periods of prayer or lengthy Bible study.

I finally realized that in that particular season of my life the best thing I could do was to meet each demand with the right attitude— doing each task for the Lord with my heart in tune to Him. Small obediences! Today, why don't you offer those little things to the Lord?

70

Since we have now been justified by his blood, how much more shall we be saved from God's wrath through him!

ROMANS 5:9

YOU CAN KNOW

Do you truly know that God has forgiven you for *all* the wrong you've ever done? You can know—beyond the shadow of a doubt!

Most of us are aware that God is perfect. He has never done anything wrong. And most of us are equally aware that we have done wrong—*we are sinners*. So God has a "problem" in that He wants us to live with Him forever, but holiness and sin cannot live together. There's that issue of you and I being sinners.

That is exactly the reason why Jesus came to earth—to live with us and die and pay the price for our sins. We should have been the ones crucified on the cross because we've sinned. We should have been the ones to pay the penalty of death. But Jesus died in our place.

The apostle Paul wrote, "Since we have now been justified by his blood, how much more shall we be saved from God's wrath through him" (Romans 5:9)! Did you notice the phrase "justified by His blood"? That means that with His blood Jesus paid for our sins so that we don't have to. By simply believing in what He did for us, we find eternal life and full forgiveness. We don't have to pretend we never did anything wrong. We don't have to cover up our sins. And, we don't have to catch God in a good mood for Him to forgive us. Forgiveness is based on a fact of history—Jesus' death on the cross for us—not on any frame of mind.

Don't spend another day wondering if you have forgiveness. Place your faith in what Jesus did on the cross. You can know that you are forgiven.

71

Teach us to number our days,
that we may gain a heart of wisdom.
PSALM 90:12

THE DEATH CLOCK

Among the strangest of websites is Deathclock.com. When you visit that site, you will be greeted with the message, "Welcome to the Death Clock, the Internet's friendly reminder that life is slipping away. . . second by second. The Death Clock will remind you just how short life is."

You can type in your birth date, gender, weight, height, and, interestingly, you need to specify whether you are a smoker or non-smoker, and also your general outlook in life. The Death Clock will then give you a "guesstimate" of your day of death, down to exactly how many seconds you have left to live. (The date is purely a guess based on life expectancy tables.) Then the number runs down before your eyes.

Why contemplate the shortness of life? One Bible verse answers that question. Moses prayed, "Teach us to number our days, that we may gain a heart of wisdom" (Psalm 90:12). I wrote down the estimated date of my death, not because I believe it's accurate but to remind myself that each day is God's gift to be used wisely.

I want to encourage you to live today fully, appreciating each moment. Anna Lindsay said, "That we are alive today is proof positive that God has something for us to do today."[1] Don't waste precious seconds in bitterness or feeling sorry for yourself. Don't let anger or revenge rob you of even one day. Life is much too priceless for that.

Today God has given you 86,400 seconds. Embrace the day, and with a wise heart, use those seconds to make a difference.

[1]Quoted in *Joy and Strength,* ed. Mary Wilder Tileston, (Boston, Massachusetts: Little, Brown, and Company, 1901), 47.

72

But the fruit of the Spirit is. . .self-control.
GALATIANS 5:22–23
(THE WHOLE STORY: GALATIANS 5:16–26)

SELF-DISCIPLINE

I was taking care of our daughter's four children by myself. Because the oldest was six and the twins were one-year-olds, I needed eyes in the back of my head to keep up with them! While I was upstairs helping three of them get dressed, one of the twins decided he would help me by pouring his own orange juice for breakfast. He managed to open the refrigerator and drag the half-gallon carton of juice from the shelf. You've already guessed what happened. As he poured the juice into his cup, the weight shifted in the carton, and soon *all* the juice was on the floor. I can't remember how many times I washed the sticky floor that day, trying to get it clean.

I have found from my experience as mother of three and grandmother of eight that I need self-discipline—lots of it—when everything is hectic. Self-discipline makes the difference between exasperation and restraint, between lashing out in impatience and controlling my anger.

But, frankly, the thought of self-discipline turns me off. I immediately think of a strait-jacket—of spending my days only thinking, *What is the next thing I must do?* How am I supposed to live that way?

The truth of the matter is that self-discipline, or self-control, is part of the fruit of the Spirit listed in Galatians 5. The fruit of the Spirit are qualities that God's Holy Spirit produces in our lives. I can no more produce self-discipline in my life by my own efforts than I can tie an apple on a tree and expect it to grow. God has to do it.

Ask God to fill you with His Spirit and strengthen you to obey Him. Then you will find self-discipline becoming more and more a natural part of your life.

73

"The King will reply, 'Truly I tell you, whatever you did for one of the least of these brothers and sisters of mine, you did for me.'"

MATTHEW 25:40

(THE WHOLE STORY: MATTHEW 25:31–40)

DO IT FOR ME

In the first months when Anita Septimus began caring for babies with AIDS, she wanted to quit. Three of the babies had already died. *Why go on with such painful work? What difference did my love and intervention make if the babies died anyway?* she asked herself. "You have not chosen a pretty profession," friends reminded her.

But Anita didn't give up. She continued to minister not only to the children but to their families. She taught them how to prevent AIDS so that other family members wouldn't contract it. She grieved with them as only parents can grieve when they lose a child.

Anita continued her labor of love to more

than three hundred families of children with AIDS. When one of the babies who would have died without her intervention celebrated her tenth birthday, Anita knew her work was worthwhile. Since 1985 Anita has devoted herself to this life-giving ministry.

She lived out her life, following what Jesus taught. "Truly I tell you," said Jesus, "Whatever you did for one of the least of these brothers and sisters of mine, you did for me" (Matthew 25:40).

Jesus said that one day we will stand before His presence to receive rewards for what we have done. If you are going through the monotony of helping someone who doesn't show appreciation, and you feel like you're wasting your time, remember that God is watching. He's keeping a record of your kindness. Keep on going, and one day you will hear Jesus tell you those words Himself.

74

*You were running a good race. Who cut in
on you to keep you from obeying the truth?*
GALATIANS 5:7

WHO CUT IN ON YOU?

The 3,000-meter women's race in the 1984
Los Angeles Olympics turned out to be
one of the most dramatic moments in sports
history. Favored to win the gold medal was
American Mary Decker. A strong competitor
was Zola Budd, the young, barefoot-running,
record-breaking athlete originally from South
Africa, now running for Great Britain.

Shortly after the halfway point of the
race, Budd and Decker collided. Decker
crashed down onto the inner field, clutching
her right thigh in pain. Budd recovered her
balance and continued with the race amidst
the booing of the crowd who thought she
had intentionally tripped Decker. Budd, who
was leading when the race began, finished
seventh. Decker was carried off the track in
tears, unable to finish the race.

Every time I hear that story, it reminds me of a verse in the book of Galatians. Young Galatian Christians were being sidetracked from their spiritual progress by an issue in the church. The apostle Paul asked them, "You were running a good race. Who cut in on you to keep you from obeying the truth?" (Galatians 5:7).

We're very much like those Galatians. We allow conflicts and disappointments with people to throw us off course. Sometimes, all it takes is for someone to bump into us with criticism and we're ready to quit. I think Paul would have also said to us, "You were running a good race. Who cut in on you?" No matter who hurts or disappoints you, it's not enough reason to quit. Take heart. Get up, refocus, and keep running.

75

*"For I know the plans I have for you," declares
the LORD, "plans to prosper you and not to
harm you, plans to give you hope and a future."*
JEREMIAH 29:11

CELEBRATE YOUR FEMININITY

Have you ever seriously thought that your being a woman and not a man is God's distinct plan for you? If God needed another man in the world, you would have been one, for there are about 104 boy babies born for every 100 girl babies. " 'For I know the plans I have for you,' declares the LORD, 'plans to prosper you and not to harm you, plans to give you hope and a future' " (Jeremiah 29:11).

Since your gender is not an accident but God's direct, individual plan for you, I encourage you to celebrate your femininity and not let anything steal your pride or enjoyment of His gift of womanhood. God gave you a beautiful body in spite of how media and today's culture have endeavored to make you feel deficient and in need of "fixing" with Botox injections and surgery. We came from the drawing board of heaven to be lovely creations of God's handiwork. Appreciate your body. Take good care of it with proper nutrition and enough exercise. Enjoy pretty clothes and feminine things.

Shortly after we were married, Harold and I visited France. I had heard about the prostitutes in Paris, but I was not prepared to see how beautiful they were—well groomed, slender, stylish, and walking with pride. "If they can look like that while making their living in that disgraceful, exploitative way," I thought, "I can keep myself attractive for my wonderful husband who is faithful to me and loves me with all his heart."

Enjoy your femininity not extravagantly or with self-centeredness, but with freedom to be the woman God has created you to be.

76

*Jesus said, "Truly I tell you, this poor
widow has put more into the treasury than
all the others. They all gave out of their wealth;
but she, out of her poverty, put in everything—
all she had to live on."*

MARK 12:43–44

(THE WHOLE STORY: MARK 12:41–44)

THE MOST VALUABLE
DONATION EVER GIVEN

O ne day, Jesus was sitting near the temple
in Jerusalem, watching the people as they
put their money into an offering box placed
close to the entrance. He noticed that many
rich people put in large amounts. But then a
poor widow came and put in two very small
copper coins worth only a fraction of a penny.

Calling His disciples to Him, Jesus said,
"Truly I tell you, this poor widow has put
more into the treasury than all the others. They
all gave out of their wealth; but she, out of her
poverty, put in everything—all she had to live
on" (Mark 12:43–44).

The other day I got to thinking about how much money has been given to the Lord's work as a result of this widow's example. We don't even know her name, but no doubt millions of dollars have been given because of her willingness to give all she had. Her tiny gift has been multiplied countless times. Wouldn't she be surprised if she knew?

Jesus still sees what we give. He knows how much we give and how much we have left after we give. He also knows our motive for giving. He looks at our hearts and knows whether we do it for Him or only to impress other people—or perhaps to assuage feelings of guilt about how blessed we really are.

Yes, God sees when you sacrifice in order to give to Him. And one day He will reward you. Give—you never know how your example will influence others.

77

For since the creation of the world God's invisible qualities—his eternal power and divine nature—have been clearly seen, being understood from what has been made, so that people are without excuse.

ROMANS 1:20

DR. NADIA

Nadia Panchenko was a shining inspiration to me. A doctor of biology, Nadia was the director of the Medico-Ecological Center in Ukraine, which researched health problems that developed from the nuclear disaster at Chernobyl. One of the first to help victims after the meltdown, Dr. Nadia refused to stop her mission in order to protect herself. As a result, she incurred high doses of radiation and her own life was shortened by cancer.

But in the intervening years, Dr. Nadia operated a clinic in Kiev to treat the people who had been relocated there from the radiation area. She cared for them for free since they had no money to pay. Children especially touched her heart because she knew they would suffer ever increasing health problems during their lifetime.

Dr. Nadia authored more than ninety scientific publications and held patents for ten discoveries relating to the blood. If she had sought popularity and status, she could have become world famous—but instead, she stayed with those who needed her most. Growing up in the former USSR, Dr. Nadia had learned only atheistic evolution. But when she began to study blood cells, she became amazed at the precision, order, and interdependence of processes in the cells. "The blood cell 'witnessed' to me about the Creator," she said. This ultimately led her to faith in Christ.

Dr. Nadia discovered the Creator in His creation. "For since the creation of the world God's invisible qualities—his eternal power and divine nature—have been clearly seen, being understood from what has been made . . ." (Romans 1:20). Her faith, in turn, made her reach out to those who so desperately needed help. Yes, Dr. Nadia, your life truly is still an inspiration!

78

*"Blessed is the one whose sin the
Lord will never count against them."*

Romans 4:8

Forgiving Yourself

The woman wept as she said, "What I
have done is so awful! I can accept that
God has forgiven me, but I can never forgive
myself." Sadly, she was setting herself up for a
lifetime of misery.

Many people don't understand the
concept of forgiveness. When God forgives,
He does not merely say, "What you did is not
so bad—and besides, I love you; I won't hold
this sin against you this time." No, that's not
what forgiveness is. Sin is bad and forgiveness
was costly. It took the death of Jesus on the
cross to pay the penalty for our sin. When God
forgives us, He does so not because He "feels"
like forgiving us. He forgives us based solidly
on the fact that Jesus paid the sentence for sin
so that we don't have to pay.

Why, then, do people not forgive themselves? My friend Dr. Richard Smith, who counsels people with forgiveness issues, says that in his experience, the people who have problems forgiving themselves don't really understand that God has fully forgiven them. God no longer looks on us as sinners but as saints, the biblical term for believers forgiven by Jesus Christ. And if that is the way God sees us, what right do we have to see ourselves in any other way? In God's eyes our sins no longer exist. Romans 4:8 says, "Blessed is the one whose sin the Lord will never count against them"

Forgiven sin is gone forever! You are wasting your time punishing yourself for it. More than that, you are dishonoring God who paid the price for your forgiveness. It's time to let your guilt feelings go! Time to forget what is behind, as Paul said, and press toward what is ahead (Philippians 3:13). Go to God in prayer and ask Him to help you finally, fully forgive yourself, now.

79

*But be sure to fear the L*ORD *and serve him
faithfully with all your heart; consider what
great things he has done for you.*

1 SAMUEL 12:24

(THE WHOLE STORY: 1 SAMUEL 12:19–24)

WHEN YOU'VE WRONGED GOD

The people of Israel wanted a king so they
could be like the pagan nations around
them. At the time they were a theocracy—a
government with God as the head and human
judges to advise the people.

But now they wanted a monarchy because
everybody else had one. In effect they said,
"God, You're not good enough for us." They
made a serious mistake.

Samuel, their judge at the time, helped them
restore their relationship with God. What he
said to them in 1 Samuel 12 gives us a pattern to
follow when we have wronged the Lord:

1. First, admit your wrongdoing. The
people said to Samuel, "We have added

to all our other sins the evil of asking for a king" (verse 19).

2. Second, turn with all your heart to the Lord.

3. Third, understand that when you repent, God will restore you. Samuel said, "For the sake of his great name the LORD will not reject his people, because the LORD was pleased to make you his own" (verse 22).

4. Fourth, let mature Christians pray for you, and humbly accept their instruction. Samuel said, "As for me, far be it from me that I should sin against the LORD by failing to pray for you. And I will teach you the way that is good and right" (verse 23).

5. Finally, thank God for His forgiveness and determine to serve Him. "Be sure to fear the LORD and serve him faithfully with all your heart," said Samuel (verse 24).

When we have wronged God, it's not the end. In fact, it can be a new beginning if we turn back to the Lord.

80

*"I called but you did not answer,
I spoke but you did not listen."*

ISAIAH 65:12

ANSWERING AND LISTENING

In these days of voice mail and caller ID, people often do not answer their phones until they know who is calling.

Surprisingly, there's a verse in the Bible about God calling us and not getting an answer. Isaiah 65:12 says, "I called but you did not answer, I spoke but you did not listen." How sad! Almighty God, the Creator of heaven and earth, called the people He loves, but they neither answered Him nor listened to what He had to say. In other words, they hung up on God.

Let's be honest. Has there been a time when you heard God's voice speak to you in your heart, but you didn't want to listen? So you let the call go on the answering machine, so to speak, and ignored God's voice. I admit I have done that.

How different is the way God deals with our calls. In the same chapter of Isaiah, God says, "Before they call I will answer; while they are still speaking I will hear" (verse 24). When we call God, He answers even before we call, not ignoring us like we sometimes ignore Him.

When you call God, you can be sure you'll get through to Him. David said, "In my distress I called to the LORD; I cried to my God for help. From his temple he heard my voice; my cry came before him, into his ears" (Psalm 18:6). God has no answering machine, no receptionist taking the call. Your cry comes directly to His ears.

The next time you sense God speaking to you, do Him the courtesy of answering.

81

*The LORD said to me, "You have seen
correctly, for I am watching to see
that my word is fulfilled."*
JEREMIAH 1:12

FORTY-SEVEN KINGS

We usually think of the Bible as a book that teaches us principles for living—the divine handbook for life. But sometimes we forget that the Bible is also an accurate record of history.

For instance, the historical books of the Old Testament (from Joshua to 2 Chronicles) record the names of forty-seven kings besides those who reigned in Israel and Judah. Strangely, for some 2,300 years, secular scholars did not recognize them as men who actually lived and ruled. In spite of these rulers' greatness, the scholars relegated them to the sphere of mythology because they simply had not found evidence outside the Bible that they had actually existed.

But archaeologists began to make new

discoveries. One by one these kings made their appearance in universally accepted historical records. Now all forty-seven of them have been authenticated by archaeological evidence. Each king has been recognized as a person who lived and ruled, just as the Bible says he did.

Aren't you glad that the words God inspired the writers of the Bible to record are true and reliable? That's a wonderful comfort when you're going through difficult times. The God who made sure that history was recorded accurately in the Bible is the same God who promises, in that same Bible, that "The LORD himself goes before you and will be with you; he will never leave you nor forsake you. Do not be afraid; do not be discouraged" (Deuteronomy 31:8).

You can rest on His promises for He said, "I am watching to see that my word is fulfilled" (Jeremiah 1:12).

82

*This inheritance is kept in heaven for you,
who through faith are shielded by God's
power until the coming of the salvation that
is ready to be revealed in the last time.*

1 PETER 1:4–5

(THE WHOLE STORY: 1 PETER 1:3–9)

GOOD THINGS IN HEAVEN

Armin Gesswein was a godly man known for prayer—and coffee. He not only led the prayer support for some of Billy Graham's early crusades, but he spent almost his entire life teaching and preaching about prayer.

Much of his life Armin ministered in Norway. There, he married a beautiful Norwegian girl, Reidun. Armin and Reidun both deeply enjoyed cups of hot, strong coffee.

They're with the Lord now, but I often exchange e-mails with their daughters, Carol and Sonja. In one exchange with Carol I mentioned that it would be great if we could get together for a cup of coffee. Since she lives many miles from where I live, I casually added, "Maybe in heaven? Or do they drink coffee in heaven?"

Carol wrote back, "Well, my dad sure loved his coffee, and since there's no unhappiness in heaven, there must be coffee in heaven!"

I wish we could peek into heaven and see what it's like. I'm looking forward to that cup of coffee with the Gessweins.

"Our citizenship is in heaven. And we eagerly await a Savior from there, the Lord Jesus Christ" (Philippians 3:20). The apostle Peter says there's "an inheritance that can never perish, spoil or fade...kept in heaven for you" (1 Peter 1:4). John added, "No longer will there be any curse. The throne of God and of the Lamb will be in the city, and his servants will serve him. They will see his face.... And they will reign for ever and ever" (Revelation 22:3–5).

I can hardly wait!

83

*Godly men buried Stephen and mourned deeply
for him. But Saul began to destroy the church.*
ACTS 8: 2–3

(THE WHOLE STORY: ACTS 7:1–8:3)

LIFE-CHANGING POWER

The evangelist Dwight L. Moody once accepted the challenge to debate with an atheist. He agreed, however, on one condition—that the atheist produce ten or more people whose lives had been changed by atheism. Moody said, "I will have at least one hundred people on the platform who will testify to the fact that belief in Christ has changed their lives." Not able to produce even ten examples, the atheist withdrew his offer.

The apostle Paul himself was a prime example of Christ's life-changing power. When we first find him in the Bible, he is a young man named Saul watching Stephen being stoned to death. The witnesses laid their outer clothes at Saul's feet. But Saul was not merely a spectator. Scripture says he was giving approval to Stephen's death (Acts 8:1). After this, Saul himself began to go from house to house, "breathing out murderous threats" (Acts 9:1) and putting Christians in prison (Acts 9:2).

Little did he know that before he could reach Damascus, he would be forever changed by an encounter with the Lord. His vocation would be changed from persecutor to preacher, his name changed from Saul to Paul, and his heart changed from burning with the desire to see Christians dead to the willingness to give his life that others might hear the Gospel.

Paul declared, "I am not ashamed of the gospel, because it is the power of God that brings salvation to everyone who believes" (Romans 1:16). The Gospel is still powerful to change lives for all eternity.

84

"I myself said, 'How gladly would I treat you like my children and give you a pleasant land, the most beautiful inheritance of any nation.' I thought you would call me 'Father' and not turn away from following me."

JEREMIAH 3:19

CALL ME FATHER

To me, one of the most heartrending verses in the Bible is Jeremiah 3:19, where God says to His wayward people, "How gladly would I treat you like my children. . . . I thought you would call me 'Father' and not turn away from following me."

Here you have God, the Supreme Being of the universe, the Creator of all that is, yearning for a father-child relationship with us. And so He grieves. He owns everything but the affection of His children.

Many women tell me they have trouble thinking of God as their heavenly Father because they have had such despicable earthly fathers.

Rather than loving, cherishing, and encouraging them, their dads molested and abused them, or simply disappeared from their lives. They have no concept of what it is like to have a father who protects and can be depended on.

Author Hannah Whitall Smith helps us conceptualize God the Father's love:

Put together all the tenderest love you know of, the deepest you have ever felt and the strongest that has ever been poured out on you; heap on it all the love of all the loving human hearts in the world; then multiply it by infinity, and you will have a faint glimpse of the love and grace of God![1]

Clearly, God wants a relationship with us, and His Father-heart yearns for us to want to be close to Him. He says it in His Word. What can we do but believe Him?

Take a moment today to thank God for being your heavenly Father. He's waiting to hear you call His name.

[1]Melvin E. Dieter and Hallie A. Dieter, *God is Enough—Selections from Published and Unpublished Devotional Writings by Hannah Whitall Smith* (Longwood, FL: Xulon Press, 2003), 97.

85

I have been crucified with Christ and I no longer live, but Christ lives in me. The life I now live in the body, I live by faith in the Son of God, who loved me and gave himself for me.
GALATIANS 2:20

WHEN GOD INTERVENES

The three young men—Matt, Steve, and Cole—were best friends. On a trip to Las Vegas, however, they were involved in a serious car accident. Matt and Cole survived, but Steve did not.

The experience of losing their best buddy, Steve, caused Matt and Cole to bond as only those who have gone through tragedy together do. The two enjoyed riding dirt bikes, and finally they planned the big trip—an entire weekend riding in the area of an old gold mining town in the desert. Scott, a third friend, went, too.

They were down to the final ride. Matt rode his bike up the hill first—and disappeared from view. As Cole crested the hill, he saw nothing but a massive hole in the ground. Frantically he and Scott began to look for Matt, but then the horror of reality set in. Matt had fallen 780 feet straight down into an abandoned, unmarked mineshaft and did not survive.

"I could feel sorry for myself, blame God, and maybe start drinking," Cole said. "Or I could do something with my life." At twenty-one, Cole made the decision to honor Steve and Matt by living a God-centered life. He began to share his testimony at churches and schools.

Cole said, "I vowed. . .that no matter how uncomfortable it may be, if I feel the Lord calling me to do something, never again will I let an opportunity pass me by."[1] Cole can now say with Paul, "I have been crucified with Christ and I no longer live, but Christ lives in me" (Galatians 2:20).

When God clearly intervenes in a person's life, it's for a purpose. Has He been speaking to you through the circumstances in your life? Listen to what He is telling you.

---

[1]Taken from Cole Hatter's prayer letter, 2005.

86

They said, "The land we explored devours those living in it. All the people we saw there are of great size. . . . We seemed like grasshoppers in our own eyes, and we looked the same to them."

NUMBERS 13:32–33

(THE WHOLE STORY: NUMBERS 13:16–33)

GRASSHOPPER FAITH

The people of Israel stood on the border of the land God had promised them. But before they went in, they sent an investigating committee of twelve men to assess the land.

All twelve saw that it was good; all twelve knew that God had promised to give it to them. But only two said, "We should go up and take possession of the land, for we can certainly do it" (Numbers 13:30). The other ten said, "We saw the Nephilim [giants] there. . . We seemed like grasshoppers in our own eyes" (Numbers 13:33).

My dad used to say, "I don't think any child of God ought to think of himself as a grasshopper. You and I have been redeemed with the precious blood of the Lord Jesus Christ. I believe in humility, but being humble does not mean showing disrespect for what God has done for you."

The ten spies reported, "The cities are large, with walls up to the sky" (Deuteronomy 1:28). Do you know why they thought that? "Because they were grasshoppers," my dad would say. "Just imagine a grasshopper down at the base of a walled city. He turns his eyes enough to look up at that wall, and it goes up, up, up, and never stops until it touches the sky. That's a grasshopper's view of a wall."

Are you facing giants and walled cities? How are you looking at them—from a grasshopper's viewpoint? God looks down from heaven and sees the same giants and the same walls, but from His vantage point they don't look very big. Be encouraged: Our God is bigger than anything we will ever face.

87

The fruit of that righteousness will be peace;
its effect will be quietness and confidence forever.
Isaiah 32:17

No More Guilty Feelings

A young woman we'll call Beth was listening to Guidelines' *Commentary* on radio when God reminded her of the shoplifting she had done thirteen years before. She knew God wanted her to make restitution.

The shoplifting had occurred when Beth switched the box of the item she was buying with that of a cheaper item. Over the years, however, whenever she recalled what she had done, she felt guilty.

When she went back to the store, however, to pay for what she had stolen, the store staff would not accept her money because it would throw off their accounting system. So Beth sent a letter with a check for the amount she owed to the general manager of the company, explaining how this had happened when she had fallen away from her Christian faith. Having asked for forgiveness from the Lord, she wrote that she felt a deep conviction that she should make restitution.

Beth received a letter from the company praising her for her honesty and saying that her check would be donated to a charity. Then they added that because her letter was such a wonderful contrast to the letters they usually received, they would frame it and hang it on their office wall. Beth says that she finds it embarrassing to picture her confession hanging on a wall, but if it brings glory to the Lord, it's okay with her. She says, "I am finally at peace."

The Bible tells us, "The fruit of that righteousness will be peace; its effect will be quietness and confidence forever" (Isaiah 32:17). Is God speaking to you about anything in your past you need to settle so you will be free from guilty feelings?

88

*I press on toward the goal to win
the prize for which God has called
me heavenward in Christ Jesus.*

PHILIPPIANS 3:14

SUCCESS OR SIGNIFICANCE?

It's exciting that many people in the world
are thinking about their life purpose since
reading Rick Warren's bestselling 2002 book
The Purpose-Driven Life.

Are you one of those who have discovered
their life purpose? Are you pursuing success or
significance?

Many of us think that in order to be
significant, we have to accomplish something
great that makes us famous. In reality, many
famous people have never accomplished
significance, and conversely, some significant
people are unknown outside the walls of their
home or organization.

If you're feeling unsuccessful or
insignificant, be encouraged to know that your

goal in life should not be to pursue what the world says is important, but to be what God says is valuable. Endeavor to take hold not of someone else's reason for being, but of God's purpose for *you*. Your job is to "press on toward the goal" (Philippians 3:14) of God's purpose for you and to leave the rest to Him.

In *Dear God, It's Me Again!* Gail Ramsey reminds us of the *Peanuts* cartoon where Charlie Brown holds out his hands to Lucy and says, "Look at these hands! These hands may someday build big bridges! These hands might hit home runs! These hands could one day write important books, or heal sick people. . .or drive a rocket ship to Mars!" Looking at Charlie Brown's hands, Lucy retorts, "They've got jelly on 'em."[1]

Lucy didn't see what Charlie Brown saw. She saw only the jelly. When others look at you, many will see just the jelly. But don't let that destroy the dream that God has put in your heart. Live out His purpose for you.

[1]Gail Ramsey, *Dear God, It's Me Again!* (New Kensington, PA: Whitaker House, 2004), 79.

89

Be strong and take heart,
all you who hope in the LORD.
PSALM 31:24

ATTITUDE MAKES
ALL THE DIFFERENCE

A delightful ninety-two-year-old lady who was legally blind was moving to a nursing home. Her husband of seventy years had recently passed away. As she maneuvered her walker to the elevator, the staff member accompanying her described her tiny room.

"I love it!" she stated with the enthusiasm of an eight-year-old who had been given a new puppy.

"Mrs. Jones, you haven't seen the room," the staff member said.

"That doesn't have anything to do with it," she replied. "Happiness is something you decide on ahead of time. Whether I like my room or not doesn't depend on how the furniture is arranged—it's how I arrange my mind. I've already decided to love it. It's a decision I make every morning when I wake up. I have a choice: I can spend the day in bed recounting the difficulty I have with the parts of my body that no longer work, or get out of bed and be thankful for parts that do. Each day is a gift, and as long as I live, I'll focus on the new day."

What a beautiful attitude to have! I'm sure we all hope that in the final years of our lives we'll reflect the positive mind-set of this dear lady.

One of the best things we can do to prepare for our golden years is to look to God as our source of hope. The God who has been faithful to us will not abandon us in the years to come. The psalmist wrote, "Be strong and take heart, all you who hope in the LORD" (Psalm 31:24), for each day is a gift from Him to be enjoyed.

90

The Lord is full of compassion and mercy.
JAMES 5:11

MERCY

A woman had her picture taken by a photographer. When she went back to see the proofs and make her selection for the final portrait, she was very disappointed with the pictures.

"Sir, these pictures do not do me justice!" she exclaimed.

"Madam, it's not justice you need but mercy."

We laugh at that, but honestly, we're all in the same position. Because we have sinned and none of us is perfect, we need mercy, not justice. And when we come to God for mercy, we have come to the right source. The Bible says, "The Lord is full of compassion and mercy" (James 5:11).

God's mercy refers to His tender caring, His forgiveness and amazing kindness toward undeserving men and women.

Even if you think your sin is too great for God to forgive, think again! The psalmist wrote, "Let the wicked forsake their ways and the unrighteous their thoughts. Let them turn to the LORD, and he will have mercy on them, and to our God, for he will freely pardon" (Isaiah 55:7). For "The LORD is compassionate and gracious, slow to anger, abounding in love. He will not always accuse, nor will he harbor his anger forever; he does not treat us as our sins deserve or repay us according to our iniquities" (Psalm 103:8–10).

You and I can find God's mercy whenever we need it. "Let us then approach God's throne of grace with confidence, so that we may receive mercy and find grace to help us in our time of need" (Hebrews 4:16). Thank God today for His bountiful mercy!

We would love to hear from you!

Please share with us how this book has
helped or blessed you. Or for additional
needs, contact Darlene Sala at

Guidelines International Ministries
Box G
Laguna Hills, California 92654,
USA

Or by e-mail at
darlene@guidelines.org